Pride and Prejudice

by Jane Austen

Shelagh Hubbard

Series Editors:
Sue Bennett and Dave Stockwin

HODDER
EDUCATION
AN HACHETTE UK COMPANY

The Publishers would like to thank the following for permission to reproduce copyright material.

Photo credits

p. 9 Georgios Kollidas/Fotolia; **p. 17** TopFoto; **p. 19** AF archive/Alamy; **p. 29** TopFoto; **p. 33** AF archive/Alamy; **p. 40** ZUMA Press, Inc./Alamy; **p. 62** Billion Photos/Fotolia

Every effort has been made to trace all copyright holders, but if any have been inadvertently overlooked, the Publishers will be pleased to make the necessary arrangements at the first opportunity.

Although every effort has been made to ensure that website addresses are correct at time of going to press, Hodder Education cannot be held responsible for the content of any website mentioned in this book. It is sometimes possible to find a relocated web page by typing in the address of the home page for a website in the URL window of your browser.

Hachette UK's policy is to use papers that are natural, renewable and recyclable products and made from wood grown in sustainable forests. The logging and manufacturing processes are expected to conform to the environmental regulations of the country of origin.

Orders: please contact Bookpoint Ltd, 130 Park Drive, Milton Park, Abingdon, Oxon OX14 4SE. Telephone: (44) 01235 827720. Fax: (44) 01235 400454. Email education@bookpoint.co.uk Lines are open from 9 a.m. to 5 p.m., Monday to Saturday, with a 24-hour message answering service. You can also order through our website: www.hoddereducation.co.uk

ISBN: 978 1 4718 5365 4

© Shelagh Hubbard, 2016

First published in 2016 by

Hodder Education,

An Hachette UK Company

Carmelite House

50 Victoria Embankment

London EC4Y 0DZ

www.hoddereducation.co.uk

Impression number   10 9 8 7 6 5 4 3 2 1

Year   2020 2019 2018 2017 2016

Cover photo: green door © Villedieu Christophe/Hemera/Thinkstock/Getty Images; keyhole © Maksim Kostenko/123RF.com

Typeset in 11/13pt Bliss Light by Integra Software Services Pvt. Ltd., Pondicherry, India

Printed in Italy

A catalogue record for this title is available from the British Library.

Contents

Getting the most from this guide

This guide is designed to help you raise your achievement in your examination response to *Pride and Prejudice*. It is intended for you to use throughout your GCSE English literature course: it will help you when you are studying the novel for the first time and also during your revision.

The following features have been used throughout this guide to help you focus your understanding of the novel.

Target your thinking

A list of **introductory questions** labelled by Assessment Objective is provided at the beginning of each chapter to give you a breakdown of the material covered. They target your thinking, in order to help you work more efficiently by focusing on the key messages.

Build critical skills

These boxes offer an opportunity to consider some **more challenging questions**. They are designed to encourage deeper thinking, analysis and exploratory thought. Building and practising critical skills in this way will give you a real advantage in the examination.

GRADE *FOCUS*

It is possible to know a novel well and yet still underachieve in the examination if you are unsure what the examiners are looking for. The **GRADE FOCUS** boxes give a clear explanation of **how you may be assessed**, with an emphasis on the criteria for gaining a Grade 5 and a Grade 8.

REVIEW YOUR LEARNING

At the end of each chapter you will find this section to **test your knowledge**: a series of short, specific questions to ensure that you have understood and absorbed the key messages of the chapter. Answers to the 'Review your learning' questions are provided in the final section of the guide (p. 109).

GRADE *BOOSTER*

Read and remember these pieces of helpful **grade-boosting advice**. They provide top tips from experienced teachers and examiners who can advise you on what to do, as well as what *not* to do, in order to maximise your chances of success in the examination.

Key quotation

Key quotations are highlighted for you, so that if you wish you may use them as **supporting evidence** in your examination answers. Further quotations, grouped by characterisation, key moments and theme, can be found in the 'Top ten' section on page 101 of the guide. All page references in this guide refer to the Penguin edition of *Pride and Prejudice* (ISBN 978-0-14-062022-1).

'You never see a fault in anybody.'
Elizabeth of Jane (Ch. 4, p. 14)

Introduction

Studying the text

You may find it useful to dip into this guide in sections as and when you need them, rather than reading it from start to finish. For example, the section on 'Context' can be read before you read the novel itself, since it offers an explanation of the relevant historical, cultural and literary background to the text. In 'Context' you will find information about aspects of Austen's life and times that influenced her writing; the particular issues with which she was concerned; and where the novel stands in terms of the literary tradition to which it belongs.

The relevant 'Plot and structure' sections in this guide could be helpful to you either before or after you read each chapter of *Pride and Prejudice*. As well as a summary of events there is also commentary on the author's methods, so that you are aware of both the key events and the literary features in each part of the novel. Later, the sections on 'Characterisation', 'Themes' and 'Language, style and analysis' will help develop your thinking further, in preparation for written responses on particular aspects of the text.

Many students also enjoy the experience of being able to bring something extra to their classroom lessons in order to be 'a step ahead of the game'. Alternatively, you may have missed a classroom session or feel that you need a clearer explanation, and the guide can help you with this too.

An initial reading of the section on 'Assessment Objectives and skills' will enable you to make really effective notes in preparation for your written answers, because you will have a very clear understanding of what the examiners are looking for. The Assessment Objectives are what examination boards base their mark schemes on. In this section the AOs are broken down and clearly explained.

Revising the text

Whether you study the novel in a block of time close to the exam or much earlier in your GCSE English literature course, you will need to revise thoroughly if you are to achieve the very best grade that you can.

Reading this guide should, of course, never be a substitute for reading *Pride and Prejudice* itself, but it can help. You should first remind yourself of what happens in the novel, and for this the chapter on 'Plot and structure' might be revisited in the first instance. You might then look at the 'Assessment Objectives and skills' section to ensure that you understand what the examiners are, in general, looking for.

'Tackling the exams' then gives you useful information on the exams and on question format, depending on which examination board specification you are following, as well as advice on the examination format, and practical considerations such as the time available for the question and the Assessment Objectives that apply to it.

Advice is also supplied on how to approach the question, writing a quick plan, and 'working' with the text, since all of the examination boards use an extract-based question for *Pride and Prejudice*. Focused advice on how you might improve your grade follows, and you need to read this section carefully.

You will find examples of exam-style responses in the 'Sample essays' section, with an examiner's comments in the margins so that you can see clearly how to move towards a Grade 5, and how then to move from a Grade 5 to a Grade 8. When looking at the sample answers, bear in mind that the way they are assessed is similar (but not identical) across the boards. It is sensible to look online at the sample questions and materials from the particular board that you are taking, and to try planning answers to as many questions as possible. You might also have fun inventing and answering additional questions, since you can be sure that the ones in the sample materials will not be the ones you see when you open the exam paper!

This guide should help you to clarify your thinking about the novel, but it is not a substitute for your thoughtful reading and discussion of *Pride and Prejudice*. The guide should also help you consolidate your approach to writing well under the pressure of the examination. The suggestions in the guide can help you to develop habits of planning and writing answers that take the worry out of *how* you write, and so enable you to concentrate on *what* you write.

The guide is intended to complement the work you do with your teacher, not to replace it. At the end of the main sections there are 'Review your learning' questions to support your thinking. There are 'Build critical skills' and 'Grade booster' boxes at various points; these help you to develop the critical and analytical skills you need to achieve a higher grade. There is also a 'Top ten' quotations section, for characters, key moments and themes. Now that all GCSE literature examinations are 'closed book', this 'Top ten' section will prove helpful in offering you the opportunity to learn short quotations to support points about characters, key moments and themes, as well as being a revision aid.

When writing about the novel, use this guide as a springboard to develop your own ideas. You should not read this guide in order to memorise chunks of it, ready to regurgitate in the exam. Examiners are not looking for set responses; identical answers are dull. They would like to see that you have used everything you have been taught — including by this guide — as a starting point for your own thinking. The examiners hope to reward you for perceptive thought, individual appreciation and varying interpretations. Try to show that you have engaged with the themes and ideas in the novel and that you have explored Austen's methods with an awareness of the context in which she wrote. Above all, don't be afraid to make it clear that you have enjoyed the novel.

There have been several stage and film productions of *Pride and Prejudice* since its first radio broadcast by the BBC in 1924. More recently there have been television adaptations very much in tune with the modern viewer, notably one scripted by Faye Weldon in 1980 and another by Andrew Davies in 1995 which includes the memorable scene where Darcy confronts Elizabeth at Pemberley half-dressed and wet through. Joe Wright's 2005 feature film, starring Keira Knightley as Elizabeth Bennet, is a popular recent adaptation.

Watch and enjoy these television and film adaptations and use them to add to your interpretation of the novel, but do beware of writing about them as if they were Austen's original work. Austen was writing about her world, not creating costume drama. Enjoy referring to the guide as you study the text, and good luck in your exam.

Context

Target your thinking

- How did Jane Austen's life influence her writing? (**AO3**)
- How much are historical events an influence on the novel? (**AO3**)
- How was life for women of Jane Austen's social class different from the life of modern women? (**AO3**)
- Is the novel still relevant to modern readers? (**AO3**)

What is meant by context?

The **context** of a novel means the circumstances in which it was written — the social, historical and literary factors that influenced what the author wrote. Comments on context might also include explanation of how the original readers of a novel might have a different understanding of it than a reader today.

The social and historical context of *Pride and Prejudice* is important: Austen's world was very different from ours, two centuries later. She focuses on a privileged class of English society and she writes from a woman's perspective about relationships between her characters rather than constructing an action-packed plot. The book went through various versions at the end of the eighteenth and beginning of the nineteenth century and was eventually published in 1813.

Jane Austen's life

This is not a history book: the most important thing to know about Jane Austen's life is that she was a writer. However, there is interest in knowing something about her, and the events of the world she lived in. Reading this section will help you make better sense of aspects of the social world of *Pride and Prejudice* that are different from today's world.

▲ Jane Austen

Jane Austen was born on 16 December 1775 and died on 18 July 1817. She had six brothers and one older sister, Cassandra. Her father was a clergyman in Steventon, Hampshire, and, at times, a teacher. Although the family was on the fringes of the social class known as 'gentry', they did not have a great deal of money — like the Bennets in *Pride and Prejudice*.

Austen was offered more education than most girls at that time. She did attend school for a while, but more of her education took place in her father's library (a little like Elizabeth Bennet) alongside her brothers and extended beyond sewing, music, French and good manners which girls of her social class usually received in school.

In her teens Austen began to write plays, poems and stories; some of these still exist in notebooks she copied out at the time. Her satirical sense of humour begins to show in this early work.

As Austen grew up, she stayed at home while her brothers married and began families of their own. Neither of the sisters married: it was not uncommon for women of their background to opt for a single life rather than risk a less than perfect marriage and death in child-birth. Nevertheless, her letters to her sister hint at a romance with a man called Tom Lefroy, but this came to nothing as neither had any inherited money to make marriage possible.

The novel was still quite a new genre of literature when Austen began to write. There were other women novelists who influenced her writing — Fanny Burney's *Cecilia* (1782) is the source of the title of *Pride and Prejudice* — but attitudes to women authors were not always positive, so it was difficult for them to get work published.

In 1800 the family moved to the city of Bath, fashionable and more sophisticated than a Hampshire village. Although Austen wrote no novels during the six years she spent there, Bath is a setting found in many of her novels. It was in Bath that she received her only proposal of marriage from Harris Bigg-Wither, a man who sounds rather like a Mr Collins.

In 1805 Austen's father died, so she, her mother and sister, now financially dependent on her brothers, moved to Southampton.

Finally publishers began to take an interest in her novels: *Sense and Sensibility* was published in 1811, followed by *Pride and Prejudice* in 1813, *Mansfield Park* in 1814 and *Emma* in 1815. The novels were popular and sold well.

In 1816, Austen became ill, though she continued to write till her death in 1817. Her final novel, *Persuasion*, was published together with *Northanger Abbey* six months after her death. She was buried in Winchester Cathedral. Chawton House is now the home of the Jane Austen museum.

The role of women

Women and writing

The novel, a fictional story about invented people, was an innovation of the eighteenth century and most early novelists were male. Women generally did not have the same education as their brothers. They were taught to read and became enormous consumers of novels, but generally did not learn to write well enough for publication. There were women writing before Jane Austen and no doubt she read the work of Fanny Burney and Amelia Opie, among others, but these books were not regarded as 'great writing' in the class of male novelists.

Women and the public world

It was hard for women at this time to have their writing taken seriously. They were not meant to take an interest in the public world of great events and politics and, although many did, it was certainly not appropriate for women to write about such things. It is said that Austen often physically hid her novel writing under the pretence of writing a letter if interrupted by an outsider.

Even though Austen's subject matter was acceptable, making her writing public was not an easy task, and it was her father and brother who tried to find a publisher for her novels. Women of her class did write, but it was usually private: personal journals and letters to friends and family — nothing intended for publication. Later in the nineteenth century women who wrote novels of ideas sometimes published under men's names (for instance Mary Ann Evans wrote under the name of George Eliot) rather than face outrage at 'unsuitable' subject matter.

Austen's world of the private and personal

The world of Austen's novels is a private and domestic one, inhabited by women like herself. She never writes about the lives of servants (though they are there in the households she describes). She rarely writes about men in a situation where there are no women present: how would she know about that?

Austen never moves out into the world of public events. During the early 1800s, there was trouble in Ireland and war between England and France, yet in *Pride and Prejudice* the only reference to the military preparations against invasion by Napoleon's troops is the red-coated captains and sergeants who provide romantic interest for the young ladies, for example Mr Wickham (Ch.15, pp. 58–59).

Build critical skills

Here are some key dates in history during Austen's life:

1775:   Start of American war of independence

1789:   French Revolution

1792:   *A Vindication of the Rights of Woman* by Mary Wollstonecraft is published

1793:   France declares war on Britain

1798:   *Lyrical Ballads*, poetry by Wordsworth and Coleridge, is published

1805:   Nelson's victory at the battle of Trafalgar

1814:   Stephenson presents his steam locomotive to the public

1815:   Napoleon defeated at Waterloo

How much do you learn about great events like these from reading *Pride and Prejudice*?

The Regency world

Build critical skills

As you read *Pride and Prejudice*, ask yourself whether in Austen you see more of the witty and logical social commentary of eighteenth-century authors, like Jonathan Swift, or evidence of Romantic ideas in the characters and events she creates.

The Regency is the period of English history between the Georgians and the Victorians and takes in Austen's adult life, from the mid-1790s until the late 1830s. The name comes from the Prince Regent who took the throne from his father, King George III, in 1811 (when King George was declared unfit to rule) to his death in 1820.

The Romantic movement

At the end of the eighteenth century, literary conventions were moving away from literature that was concerned with intellectual argument and rational understanding towards writing that described strong emotions as a valid source of meaningful human experience. This is now known as the Romantic movement and it involved artists and musicians as well as writers.

Untamed nature and spontaneous emotions became the subjects of Romantic poets like Wordsworth, Shelley and Byron, whose work was both fashionable and popular in Austen's time.

A culture of revolution and freedom

Writers also celebrated events like the French Revolution, which altered thinking about class and equality, power and freedom.

Books about politics and philosophy appeared on both sides of the Channel with new ideas — even the beginnings of a proposal that women might be equal to men. Austen resisted being swept away by excitement: the balance and judgement she promotes in the novels is her response. She is wary of the Romantic attitude that emotion is a truer response to life's events than rational thought: it is very clear in her writing that characters whose hearts rule their heads end up in disastrous circumstances — as does Lydia Bennet.

Yet she allows her heroines to be unconventional in some ways: Elizabeth Bennet walks to Netherfield, hatless, and looking 'almost wild' when she arrives. She speaks to Darcy (and even the intimidating Lady Catherine) as an intellectual equal, a radical thing to do, considering the social distance between them.

▲ Elizabeth and Darcy

Fashion

The stiff clothing and powdered wigs of the early Georgians contrasted with the fashions in Regency times: soft, flowing empire-line muslin dresses for women and natural hair for both sexes. The same underlying idea of celebrating freedom and nature, as opposed to the previous generation's more formal and sophisticated approach to life, is therefore reflected in how people dressed.

Social class

Rigid social class barriers in England began to break down a little in the eighteenth century, as people whose wealth was based on ownership of land (the traditional aristocracy, like Darcy's mother's family) were joined by people who had made their money in trade and industry (as Darcy's father had done). Rich middle-class people could buy education for their sons to turn them into gentlemen (like Mr Bingley). They could even buy titles from old landed families who had fallen on hard times. A pretty girl whose family had made money might make a good marriage to an aristocrat who needed cash to maintain his ancestral home. Yet snobbery still existed against those who had earned rather than inherited money. The most severe snobbery could be shown by the children of parents who had earned the money. The Bingley sisters are an example of this.

Changes in attitude were certainly taking place in enlightened circles. In *Pride and Prejudice* demonstrations of the blurring of social divisions include:

- Darcy's friendship with Bingley
- the growth in his respect for the middle-class Gardiners
- his rift with his aristocratic aunt, Lady Catherine, when he chooses Elizabeth Bennet as his wife

Income and inheritance

Upper-class marriages were often based on considerations about money. There are examples of that in the novel. Austen's work is modern (even revolutionary) in her portrayal of the ideal marriage being between individuals who love and respect each other. These matches are 'suitable' (based on secure finances) but they involve romantic love in the modern sense of the word. Sometimes Austen's work is revolutionary in that she shows love overturning conventional expectations about age gaps or social distance.

The institution of marriage was important to the rich middle class and the gentry because all the family money, land and property were inherited by the eldest son. Girls did not usually inherit, unless there were no male heirs at all (Lady Catherine and her daughter). In fact, women rarely had any independent income. Daughters depended on their father's incomes, wives on their husbands and unmarried women on their brothers or more distant family. It was almost impossible for a middle-class woman to find any respectable way of earning her own living and there were no state benefits in those days. Marriage was therefore the only way to escape dependence on the family or poverty.

The main reason for giving almost all the land and wealth to one child was to stop great estates being broken up. There was a strict order of male inheritance: the eldest son got the big house and most of the fortune that went with it. The next son was educated and prepared for the church (a nice house and some land would go with the job as in the case of Mr Collins). Younger sons went into the army or sometimes became gentleman farmers.

If a family was rich enough, a father could give each of his children an income from the estate. In less wealthy families, the younger children had to make good marriages to ensure they had something to live on.

Entailment was a legal way of making sure houses and money went to a male. If there was no son, the nearest male relative would inherit. This is what has happened to Mr Bennet, who has no son. His cousin, Mr Collins, not the Bennet sisters, will inherit Longbourn.

Etiquette: civility and manners

To a modern reader, the world of *Pride and Prejudice* seems like a foreign country, with its unspoken rules and expectations of how people should behave. The words 'gentleman' and 'civility' are repeated through the book, both carrying expectations of standards of behaviour. The opening chapters show how visits and introductions have to be carried out in a certain way. There are rules about what is acceptable in conversation, between different ranks of society and between the sexes. Mrs Bennet, her sister, Mrs Philips, Mr Collins and Lydia all become embarrassments to Elizabeth and Jane because they fail to follow these rules.

Austen is concerned with matters of morality and constantly draws the reader's attention to rude or hypocritical behaviour. We are required to judge whether the expectations and standards themselves are valid and useful, as well as making judgements about how the characters in the book measure up to the expectations society places upon them.

GRADE *FOCUS*

Grade 5
Students will be able to show understanding of context and to comment clearly on how it is reflected in the text.

Grade 8
Students will be able to make perceptive, critical sustained comments about the ways that contextual factors affect the choices writers make.

REVIEW YOUR LEARNING

(Answers are given on p. 109.)

1 What is meant by the 'context' of a novel?
2 Why was it difficult for Austen to get her work published?
3 How did the Regency period get its name?
4 What was the Romantic movement?
5 What is meant by 'entailment'?
6 Why was money such an important element when considering marriage in Austen's era?
7 From what you know so far, does the novel seem relevant today's reader?

Plot and structure

Target your thinking

- What are the obstacles to Darcy and Elizabeth's relationship? (**AO1**)
- Which events draw them together? (**AO1**)
- How does the passage of time underpin and reflect the development of their relationship? (**AO1 and AO2**)

Pride and Prejudice is a lengthy novel of 61 chapters and nearly 300 pages. To aid your understanding of events, this guide divides the plot into eight sections.

Chapters 1–12: Bingley's first month at Netherfield

Austen opens the novel by introducing us to Mr and Mrs Bennet and their five daughters as they discuss the news that a single, wealthy young man, Mr Bingley, has rented a local estate, Netherfield Park. Mrs Bennet sees him as a potential husband for her eldest daughter, Jane.

Having visited the Bennets, Bingley goes to London and returns to the house with his two sisters, Caroline Bingley and Louisa Hurst, Louisa's husband, and his very wealthy friend, Mr Darcy, all of whom make their first appearance at a public ball in Meryton.

Build critical skills

Remember that the novel's original title was *First Impressions* as you read the description of how the girls first meet Bingley and Darcy at the Meryton assembly. Concentrate on Ch. 3, pp. 10–12 from 'Mr Bingley was good looking and gentlemanlike;' to '...Longbourn, the village where they lived...'. Two key points are highlighted here:
- How things appear and how the reality may differ becomes an important theme (see p. 54 in the 'Themes' section).
- Irony (where you as reader are made aware that some people's opinions are misguided) underlines the unreliability of general gossip or judgements.

How many examples can you find in the extract?

Key quotation

...a report soon followed that Mr Bingley was to bring twelve ladies and seven gentlemen with him to the assembly.

(Ch. 3, p. 10)

Over the next fortnight the two households meet on several occasions, memorably at Lucas Lodge where Austen shows how Darcy has changed his mind that none of the local girls is worth dancing with, and is actually attracted to Elizabeth. He is surprised when he invites her to dance and she refuses.

GRADE BOOSTER

```
A central theme is established: Darcy's
supposed pride (prompted by his
prejudice against the lower classes)
and Elizabeth's hurt pride (at his
rejection of her) prompts her prejudice
against him. Hers continues long after
he has changed his mind about his
initial judgement. Following this theme
as it develops and considering how it
applies to other characters will enable
you to reach the higher grades.
```

▲ Darcy and Bingley

Jane's closeness to the Bingleys grows and she is delighted by an invitation to Netherfield. Her mother sends her on horseback, hoping that poor weather means she will have to stay overnight. The plan works better than Mrs Bennet could wish: Jane is soaked, catches cold and has to remain there in bed for a couple of days. Elizabeth, to the horror of the Bingley sisters, walks three miles through the fields to look after her sister, arriving with a muddy petticoat and messy hair.

Whilst Jane recovers, the sisters spend the best part of a week at Netherfield. Darcy now begins to admire Elizabeth's spirited character as well as her looks — and Caroline Bingley is most put out.

Build critical skills

Read Ch. 10, pp. 42–44 from 'Mrs Hurst sang with her sister…' to the end of the chapter. Note how cleverly Austen, though writing in the third person, switches point of view here, from Elizabeth's:

'She hardly knew how to suppose that she could be an object of admiration to so great man' to Darcy's:

'…there was a mixture of sweetness and archness in her manner which made it difficult for her to affront anybody' to Caroline's:

'Miss Bingley saw, or suspected, enough to be jealous….'

By the time Elizabeth goes home, Darcy has resolved to control his feelings. However, do you think the stay has altered her opinion of him?

Chapters 13–20: Introducing Mr Collins and Mr Wickham

Mr Bennet informs the family that he has been in communication with his cousin, Mr Collins, for a month and that this young man, who is destined to inherit their estate, is coming to stay. Collins' letter marks him out as 'a mixture of servility and self-importance' (p. 52) and this is confirmed when he arrives and immediately assures the Bennets that he intends to make an offer of marriage to one of his cousins.

Elizabeth, Kitty and Lydia walk into Meryton with Collins where they meet Wickham. Elizabeth is attracted to him and is intrigued by his reaction to a chance meeting with Darcy. Mrs Bennet's sister, Aunt Philips, invites the group to a supper party where Elizabeth spends much time talking to Wickham and he tells her the history of the breakdown of his relationship with the Darcy family. Remind yourself that outward appearances can be deceptive — and that first impressions may be proved wrong.

> **Build critical skills**
>
> Read Ch. 16, pp. 62–65 from 'Mr Wickham did not play at whist...' to 'He deserves to be publicly disgraced'. What does the reader learn here?

GRADE BOOSTER

Austen's introduction of Wickham into the story influences the development of the plot: he hardens Elizabeth's prejudice against Darcy, making her less receptive to his attentions. Her attraction to him also makes it less likely that she would consider any relationship with the unattractive Mr Collins. Demonstrating understanding of the subtext and how Austen structures the plot will raise your grade.

The Bennet sisters wait impatiently for the long-promised ball at Netherfield. On their arrival, Elizabeth is disappointed to find that Wickham is not there. She is then surprised and irritated to be invited to dance by Darcy with whom she has an uncomfortable conversation about his treatment of Wickham, although no name is mentioned. As the evening progresses she is embarrassed by the behaviour of her family (see pp. 37 and 39 in the 'Characterisation' section).

Next morning, further discomfort is caused by Collins' proposal of marriage.

▲ Elizabeth and Darcy at the ball in the 2005 film

Build critical skills

Read Collins' proposal in Ch. 19, pp. 85–86, from 'Believe me my dear Miss Elizabeth...' to '...impossible for me to do otherwise than decline them'.

- Consider the order of the half-dozen reasons Collins enumerates for wishing to marry her. Why is this a particularly insulting way to begin?
- Can you find any evidence for the 'violence of [his] affection' for Elizabeth? What seems to be the personal reason for his wish to marry her?

Key quotation

'To fortune I am perfectly indifferent... one thousand pounds in the 4 per cents, which will not be yours till after your mother's decease, is all that you may ever be entitled to. On that head...I shall be uniformly silent.'

Mr Collins proposes to Elizabeth (Ch. 19, p. 86)

GRADE BOOSTER

Note Austen's use of irony (see p. 60), in that we interpret Mr Collins' words in a very different sense from the seeming tone of sincerity and rationality of what he says. Note also Mr Bennet's ironical response to the proposal on p. 90: 'Your mother will never see you again if you do not marry Mr Collins, and I will never speak to you again if you do.' Discussion of language techniques allows you to analyse and evaluate quoted evidence and will gain marks.

Chapters 21–29: Motivations for marriage

Two days after the ball, the Bingleys leave for London and Jane is upset. Elizabeth's reaction is diverted by two events. First, Wickham is back in Meryton. Second, to everyone's astonishment, two days after his proposal to Elizabeth, Collins proposes to Charlotte Lucas and is accepted.

Build critical skills

Read the final page of Ch. 22, pp. 100–01.
- How do different characters react to Charlotte's acceptance of Collins?
- What are the advantages Charlotte expects from the marriage?
- Do you agree with Elizabeth's opinion that it is impossible that Charlotte will be happy?

Austen sets slower development of the plot against the background of the cold, grey, protracted English winter. The season reflects the suspended emotions of the main characters. Almost a month passes as Jane waits for a letter from Caroline Bingley.

The letter finally arrives, stating that there is no intention to return to Netherfield. Jane is very upset despite Elizabeth's attempts to comfort and distract her.

Mrs Bennet's brother and his wife (the Gardiners) arrive at Longbourn for Christmas and Wickham is a constant guest. Mrs Gardiner is from Derbyshire and knows of the Darcy and Wickham families, though has no knowledge of the events that caused the two young men to fall out. She warns Elizabeth that a relationship with Wickham is impractical as neither has money to finance a marriage. Elizabeth draws a parallel between her own and Charlotte's circumstances.

Build critical skills

Read Ch. 28, pp. 123–24 from 'Elizabeth was prepared to see him in his glory...' to '...he must be often forgotten.' How does Austen create humour in this description and what is the effect on the reader?

Christmas over, the Gardiners return to London and Jane goes with them. Charlotte and Collins marry in the New Year, promising that Elizabeth may visit Hunsford in March.

Jane, hearing nothing from the Bingley sisters, pays them a visit at the Hursts' townhouse. They treat her coldly and, rudely, do not return her call for a month. It is clear to Elizabeth, when she reads of this in Jane's letter, that they have lost interest in her.

Spring arrives and the plot begins to quicken. Elizabeth discovers that Wickham has transferred his affections to a Miss King, who has just inherited £10,000 a year. Sir William and Maria Lucas set off with Elizabeth to visit the Collins'. They travel from Hertfordshire to Kent via the Gardiners' London house.

Mrs Gardiner discusses Wickham's change of affections and Elizabeth compares his motivation to Charlotte's, saying he has a need to consider finance when choosing a spouse. Mrs Gardiner invites Elizabeth on a summer tour 'to the lakes' and Elizabeth accepts.

From London the Lucases and Elizabeth travel on to Hunsford where Collins and Charlotte take pleasure in showing them the parsonage.

Within days they are all invited to Rosings to dine with the woman we already know from Wickham as Darcy's proud aunt, Lady Catherine de Bourgh, and her daughter, Anne, who Caroline Bingley has implied will be Darcy's wife. There is a great deal of humour at the end of this section as Elizabeth fends off Lady Catherine's arrogant interference and intrusive personal questions.

Key quotation

'No governess? How was that possible? Five daughters brought up at home without a governess?...Your mother must have been quite a slave to your education.'

Lady Catherine to Elizabeth (Ch. 29, p. 129)

Chapters 30–34: Darcy's courting of Elizabeth

Easter approaches, a time of year associated with renewed life and hope, and there is talk of Darcy visiting Rosings. Elizabeth assumes he will be with the same party as at Netherfield, so it is a surprise when Darcy arrives accompanied only by his cousin, Colonel Fitzwilliam. It is more of a surprise when the two young men return Collins' welcoming visit by calling at Hunsford the very next day. Charlotte guesses that Elizabeth is the attraction.

Build critical skills

This section is a key turning point in the plot and requires close attention. Reread chapters 30–34 and think carefully about:
- clues that Darcy is seeking out Elizabeth's company to learn more about her
- evidence that other characters guess his feelings, even though Elizabeth is blind to them

GRADE BOOSTER

Colonel Fitzwilliam serves a purpose in the plot like that of Wickham. He contrasts with Darcy, having easy manners and the ability to make interesting conversation; it is soon clear that he and Elizabeth are attracted to each other. While the scene at Rosings where Lady Catherine continuously interrupts their conversation (pp. 135-38) may be an example of comic satire, it also reveals how interested Darcy is in Elizabeth, possibly hinting at jealousy of her growing relationship with a love rival. Your ability to comment in detail like this on the author's purpose will gain you marks.

Darcy begins to seek out occasions to speak to Elizabeth on her own. The first could be an accident — he visits the Parsonage when the Lucas sisters are out. However, further meetings occur as Elizabeth takes solitary walks. She cannot understand how they keep meeting because she has told him about her enjoyment of walking to warn him away from her, but the reader can see that Darcy is actively pursuing her company.

Elizabeth's growing closeness with Colonel Fitzwilliam comes to an abrupt end when he reminds her that younger sons do not have financial independence and that he would not be able to consider taking a wife who did not bring a fortune with her. His words echo Wickham's action (the pursuit of Miss King), though his behaviour is a good deal more gentlemanly.

He reveals that Darcy has spoken of how he separated Bingley from a romance because of 'very strong objections towards the lady' (Ch. 33, p. 145), though, ironically, he has no idea it is Elizabeth and her family who would be offended by hearing of this.

Thus the circumstances of Darcy's proposal mirror those of Collins': she prefers another man (a disappointment), and once again, he has been the source of information which reinforces her prejudice against Darcy.

Build critical skills

Reread Darcy's proposal (Ch. 34, pp. 147–48) from 'While settling this point…'.to 'But it is of small importance.'
- List the reasons Darcy has 'struggled' against his feelings for Elizabeth, though note how he stresses that his love and admiration have overcome his reservations.
- Consider why Jane Austen chose to write Collins' proposal as dialogue, whilst here she paraphrases much of what Darcy says. The possible effect here is to place the reader in Elizabeth's shoes. Where does the account reflect her response rather than his words?

The chapter ends with each of the couple in a state of considerable agitation. Elizabeth's is conveyed by the author. The reader is left to guess at Darcy's.

Chapters 35–42: Reflections — and changes of heart

An important development occurs immediately after Elizabeth rejects Darcy's proposal. Austen includes a lengthy letter from him, 'two sheets of letter paper, written quite through, in a very close hand' (p. 152), from which the reader has a first real opportunity to see his character from his viewpoint.

Build critical skills

Reread Ch. 35, pp. 152–55. Then consider the first part of Darcy's letter and form your opinion of his motives for separating his friend Bingley from Jane. How does this affect the modern reader's view of him?

The reader is shown how Elizabeth gradually changes her opinion of Darcy. Initially, she resolves not to reread the letter, but in the end Austen describes it as almost falling apart from being read and reread. If you have ever received an important letter, text or email, you will understand this. We are shown how she reflects upon and reinterprets what Darcy has said over and over again. She realises how Wickham's deceptive charm blinded her to his bad character and begins to understand the true character of Darcy: her prejudice about his assumed pride has prevented her from seeing till now. She eventually has a complete change of heart.

From this **anagnorisis** onwards, Elizabeth moves closer and closer to her destiny, marriage with Darcy. Like Darcy, she begins to change for the better. In terms of development of the plot, only when that transformation of each is complete will they be ready to marry.

Elizabeth and Maria return to London, from where, with Jane, they travel to Longbourn. Austen then sets up two elements of plot that will shape the concluding sections of the novel.

First, Lydia's silly, reckless character is brought to the fore. Elizabeth points out to her father the dangers of allowing her to follow the regiment to Brighton. Cynical Mr Bennet is sure she will come to no real harm, but it is obvious to the reader that she will not be effectively chaperoned by young Mrs Forster and that trouble is bound to follow.

Second, the Gardiner's long trip to the Lake District becomes impossible, and Derbyshire is now their destination. Mrs Gardiner is delighted when the chance to return to her childhood home and a visit to Darcy's country estate at Pemberley is proposed, to Elizabeth's discomfort.

Chapters 43–48: Love and loss at Pemberley

The visit to Pemberley is a crucial turning point in the development of Elizabeth and Darcy's relationship (see pp. 32, 53 and 66 for more discussion of the significance of Pemberley as a setting). During the visit, Elizabeth's reflections on her changing judgement of Darcy are abruptly halted as she comes face to face with the man himself. Despite their mutual embarrassment, Darcy greets her with 'perfect civility', explaining that he has come ahead of a house party, including the Bingleys, who will arrive the following day.

Key quotation

She grew absolutely ashamed of herself. — Of neither Darcy nor Wickham could she think, without feeling that she had been blind, partial, prejudiced, absurd… 'Till this moment, I never knew myself.'
Elizabeth's thoughts (Ch. 36, page 162)

anagnorisis: a moment in classical drama where a character realises an important truth about themselves, which causes a major turning point in the plot

As Elizabeth resumes her tour around the grounds, she continues to reflect on her changing emotions as she reaches 'a spot less adorned than any they had yet visited; and the valley, here contracted into a glen, allowed room only for the stream, and a narrow walk amidst the rough coppice-wood which bordered it. Elizabeth longed to explore its windings...' (p. 194).

> **GRADE BOOSTER**
>
> Symbolism is used to reflect Elizabeth's wish to explore the hidden aspects of Darcy: his mind, his intellect. It may also work to suggest her interest in him physically. Understanding and exploring such a complex example of symbolism will lead to a high grade.

Darcy invites Mr Gardiner to fish and asks Elizabeth if he may introduce his sister to her. He has learnt his lesson: his conduct is perfect, his manners those of a true gentleman. He has taken Elizabeth's criticisms of his haughty attitude to heart. He brings his sister to meet Elizabeth. Darcy's sister then entertains the ladies at Pemberley whilst Darcy organises a fishing party for the men. Elizabeth is reacquainted with the Bingleys and is pleased Mr Bingley remembers the date of the Netherfield ball, the last time he saw Jane.

A dinner party is planned, but unfortunate events intervene: two letters from Jane arrive at the same time (the first having been misdirected) and Elizabeth reads them in sequence. Her worst fears have come to pass, for Lydia and Wickham have eloped.

Darcy finds Elizabeth after she has read Jane's letters. She is absolutely honest about the events and, although he seems concerned for her welfare, he says little. Elizabeth interprets his silence as an end to their closeness. She is acutely aware of the scandal of Lydia's actions and assumes that Darcy will wish to have no more to do with her family. However, there is an alternative way for the reader to interpret his silence: he experienced a similar shock when Wickham's plan to elope with his sister Georgiana was exposed. As the plot progresses, we begin to understand that his thoughts are less of himself and more of what he can do — not for Lydia or Wickham but for Elizabeth.

The Gardiners and Elizabeth return to Longbourn, from where Mr Gardiner travels immediately to London to join Mr Bennet in his search for the couple. Austen here injects elements of satirical comedy into the story as Mrs Bennet frets that her husband may be killed in a duel with Wickham. There are also exaggerated contrasts of attitude in Lydia's thoughtless note explaining her departure to Mrs Forster ('I can hardly write for laughing' p. 223) and Mr Collins' sanctimonious letter advising Mr Bennet to 'throw off your unworthy child' (p. 227).

Chapters 49–55: Darcy helps Lydia

Letters between London and Longbourn now play an important part in relating events as Mr Gardiner searches for the runaway lovers. Within a few days they are found and financial arrangements are put in place to ensure their marriage. At first it seems that Wickham has more money than suspected when he agrees to marry Lydia if she is assured of £1,000 on her father's death and £100 a year until then. Mr Bennet accepts these terms with disbelief. He reminds the reader of Wickham's previous pursuit of wealthy heiresses when he expresses surprise that anything less than £10,000 would persuade Wickham to marry — the same sum as Miss King's tempting fortune. However, their future is settled and a visit to Longbourn is planned after their wedding and before they travel to Newcastle to Wickham's new army posting.

Lydia moves to the Gardiners for a fortnight to prepare for the wedding and Elizabeth is left with time on her hands to regret that Lydia's rash actions have brought an end to her chances of a relationship with Darcy. Now that hopes of marriage have been dashed, she reflects that this could have been the perfect match for her.

A great surprise, therefore, is Lydia's careless revelation that Darcy was present at her wedding. Letters pass between Mrs Gardiner and Elizabeth in which it becomes clear how much the Bennet family owes to Darcy (as the reader may have suspected for some time).

- His knowledge of the circumstances of Wickham's planned elopement with his sister helped him to locate the couple.
- Before the Gardiners knew where the couple were staying, he bribed Wickham into marriage by:
  - paying off his debts (not for the first time)
  - buying him a commission in the regular army to remove him from the scene of the scandal in Brighton
  - doubling the sum of the settlement for Lydia to £2,000

Mrs Gardiner's letter hints that Elizabeth surely knew this, and that the reason for Darcy's actions can only be his feelings for her.

It is now almost a year since Bingley first rented Netherfield and news arrives that the house is being prepared for his return. Within days, Bingley and Darcy visit the Bennet family. A dinner party follows where the reader shares Elizabeth's frustration at her being unable to speak to Darcy at any length.

He then leaves for London as Jane and Bingley's courtship proceeds — now with his blessing. More social visits follow, during which Mrs Bennet makes an exhibition of herself in her attempts to leave the couple alone together. In the end she succeeds, Bingley proposes to Jane and she accepts.

Key quotation

She began now to comprehend that he was exactly the man who, in disposition and talents, would most suit her...

(Ch. 50, p. 239)

GRADE BOOSTER

```
How does
the repeated
proposal
structure
(see p. 46) of
disappointment
and acceptance
reflect the
experience of
both Lydia and
Jane in this
section of the
plot? How does
this impact on
the reader's
expectations
for Elizabeth
as the novel
draws to
a close?
Commenting
on aspects of
plot structure
like this will
lead to high
grades.
```

Chapters 56–61: Darcy resumes his courtship of Elizabeth

A surprise visit from Lady Catherine moves the plot forward rapidly. She has had news via the Lucases and Charlotte not only of Bingley and Jane's engagement, but also that Darcy's and Elizabeth's will follow. She is incensed at her plans for Anne being thwarted, and becomes even angrier when she cannot force Elizabeth to promise such an engagement will never happen. In fact, her visit is shown to have the reverse effect, awakening Elizabeth's hope of Darcy's continued feelings for her, though simultaneously reminding her (and the reader) of all the obstacles of social rank that stand between them.

A letter from Collins to Mr Bennet advises Elizabeth to avoid Lady Catherine's displeasure. Mr Bennet's amusement in sharing the contents with Elizabeth, since he knows nothing of her changed feelings towards Darcy, causes her further discomfort.

Build critical skills

Read Ch. 58, pp. 282–83. This is the climax of the plot: the moment the reader has been waiting for. All is quickly resolved. Elizabeth, alone with Darcy, opens up the possibility of intimate discussion by thanking him for all he did to help Lydia. Notice how Austen again chooses to write the proposal in reported speech rather than as dialogue.

How much information is given about the changes each has brought about in the other's character? Does the proposal happen as you expected?

The plot is brought to a conclusion. Bingley and Jane are delighted to hear the news. Mr Bennet is first alarmed, but Elizabeth reassures him that she is not entering into a marriage that could lead to similar unhappiness to his own. Mrs Bennet overcomes her dislike for Darcy very rapidly when she considers his wealth. (A double wedding is the conventional happy ending of a Shakespearean comedy. In following this pattern, Austen brings her plot to a resolution.)

Letters are sent to acquaint others with the news and responses are summarised, from Lady Catherine's anger to Georgiana's four-page expression of pleasure. The wedding itself is not described.

The final chapter summarises to what extent the various couples in the novel 'live happily ever after', telling how Jane and Bingley settle conveniently 'within thirty miles' (p. 297) of Pemberley. Lydia and Wickham are helped to cope with their itinerant life of debt. Life at

Pemberley is blessed with the happiness of Darcy and Elizabeth, and the friendship between Elizabeth and her sister-in-law, and the Darcys and the Gardiners. Even Lady Catherine forgives them sufficiently to visit.

The passage of time

The events of the novel take place over slightly more than a year: from September of one year to October of the next. You have to pay close attention to work this out as dates are infrequently mentioned, though there is mention of days of the week and of the time lapsing between events. Some timings are so precise it gives the impression that Jane Austen plotted events on a calendar.

GRADE FOCUS

Your exam task will never ask you to write a plot summary of the novel. However, you will need to have a sound grasp of the events and structure of the novel in order to be able to respond to AO2, which rewards analysis of the text structure.

Grade 5

Students must show a clear and detailed understanding of explicit and implicit meanings of the whole text and of the effects created by its structure. They will be able to select and comment on relevant references from the text.

Grade 8

Students' responses will display a comprehensive critical understanding of explicit and implicit meanings in the text as a whole and will examine and evaluate the writer's use of structure in detail. They will be able to select precise references and show insight in their comments.

REVIEW YOUR LEARNING

(Answers are given on pp. 109–110.)

1 During what season does the novel start and end?

2 Using the Plot and structure summary, list five major obstacles to Darcy and Elizabeth's developing love story.

3 Which three male characters are included as rivals for Elizabeth's affections and why?

4 When does Elizabeth fall in love with Darcy?

5 Why are the Gardiners important to the plot?

6 What similar experience do Lydia Bennet and Georgiana Darcy have?

7 How do the seasons reflect the development of the plot?

Characterisation

Target your thinking

- How does Austen present her characters to us? (**AO2**)
- What functions do characters serve in the novel? (**AO1 and AO2**)

Austen's methods of presenting characters can be a puzzle for new readers — she requires you to get under the surface of the evidence to interpret what it reveals about characters. There are four main types of evidence for character:

1 **Dialogue** — what the character says (or thinks) and what others say about them.

2 **Actions** — what a character does.

3 **Behaviour in a social setting** — words and actions relating to others.

4 **Authorial comment** — how the author explains or judges the character.

> **GRADE** *BOOSTER*
>
> ```
> Characters are constructs of the author. Beware of
> writing about them as if they are real people. Your
> ability to evaluate how characters are presented
> depends on your interpretation of their dialogue,
> actions, behaviour and authorial comment. Work on
> deepening your knowledge and understanding of these
> aspects to gain high marks.
> ```

Elizabeth Bennet

Austen's heroine is introduced into the story in her father's words as 'my little Lizzy', indicating to us that he favours her above her elder sister, Jane, the conventionally pretty one. As events add to our understanding, we see that this is because she is the daughter with a good intellect, the one he treats almost like a son. First impressions of Elizabeth are built up by dialogue — conversations between her father and mother as they talk of the arrival of the eligible Mr Bingley in the neighbourhood.

Key quotation

'They have none of them much to recommend them...they are all silly and ignorant like other girls; but Lizzy has something more of quickness than her sisters.'

Mr Bennet of his daughters (Ch. 1, p. 6)

Austen also invites us to judge Elizabeth from what she says herself: her very first utterance shows her to be more adult and aware of social form than either of her parents seems to be:

> 'But you forget, mama,' said Elizabeth, 'that we shall meet him at the assemblies, and that Mrs. Long has promised to introduce him.'

> 'I do not believe Mrs. Long will do any such thing. She has two nieces of her own. She is a selfish, hypocritical woman, and I have no opinion of her.'

> (Ch. 2, p. 7)

Her mother is shown to be impetuous and self-centred, while we see Elizabeth sweetly reminding her how the introduction to their new neighbours may be made, maintaining all 'civility' (an important word indicating how well a person may be judged in and by their own society).

A lively, playful disposition

A great deal will always be revealed once characters are placed into a social setting. These settings punctuate the story, the first being the public ball at Meryton. Here Elizabeth reacts to Darcy's slight by mocking him, though Austen chooses to use her authorial voice to summarise what Elizabeth *does*, rather than reporting the words she says.

▲ Darcy's slight to Elizabeth

Key quotation

Mr. Darcy walked off; and Elizabeth remained with no very cordial feelings towards him. She told the story, however, with great spirit among her friends; for she had a lively, playful disposition, which delighted in anything ridiculous.

(Ch. 3, p. 12)

What she *feels* about the man or his remark is not explicitly stated. However, Austen makes us aware of Elizabeth's attractive qualities by analysing Darcy's feelings about her:

> …no sooner had he made it clear to himself and his friends that she had hardly a good feature in her face, than he began to find it was rendered uncommonly intelligent by the beautiful expression of her dark eyes …

> (Ch. 6, p. 20)

Key quotation

'I might as well inquire,' replied she, 'why, with so evident a design of offending and insulting me, you chose to tell me that you liked me against your will, against your reason, and even against your character? Was not this some excuse for incivility, if I was uncivil?'

Elizabeth rejects Darcy's offer of marriage (Ch. 34, p. 149)

Confident in any company

Austen also employs dialogue to demonstrate how Elizabeth succeeds in standing up to the unpleasant and ill-mannered comments of Caroline Bingley during her stay at Netherfield (see pp. 61–62 in 'Language, style and analysis' for a detailed discussion). In conversation with Darcy, she more than holds her own in terms of both subject matter and wit. The education she is said to have received at her father's hands has been effective.

As Austen advances the story, she develops Elizabeth's good qualities, presenting her as caring and loyal. She guards her sister, Jane, as far as she can from hurt, as her mother should but does not. She is generally perceptive and a good judge of character, demonstrated by her reaction to Collins' proposal. However, Austen also shows how Elizabeth is fooled by the superficial 'most gentlemanlike appearance' (Ch.15, p. 58) of handsome, charming Wickham. Flattered by the way he singles her out for attention, her prejudice (and indeed pride) lead her to react in a way that contrasts completely with her reaction to Darcy.

Austen presents more of Elizabeth's spirited character when she stands up to Darcy's arrogant aunt, Lady Catherine de Bourgh. We are also invited to empathise with her horror when Darcy makes a proud and reluctant proposal of marriage.

Able to admit she was wrong

Austen shows us how, through mature reflection, Elizabeth comes to realise that she has badly misjudged Darcy's character, especially when she visits Pemberley. The house is constructed as a symbol of the man, and we see how Elizabeth begins to fall in love. She learns that she has jumped to conclusions and misjudged Darcy, and that her intelligence does not make her immune from mistakes (see pages 23–24, 53 and 66 for further discussion of the visit to Pemberley).

Ultimately we see her grow up. By the end, her pride has been challenged and her prejudice eliminated by learning the truth about the man she loves. Their relationship has made a better human being out of each of them, a fundamental in a good pairing by Austen's judgement. They marry. Elizabeth is rewarded with the love of a very rich man and a wonderful home, but equally we are shown how she shares the good fortune and her good influence with those around her. The novel does not end at the altar; the final chapter shows how her generosity benefits Georgiana Darcy, the Wickhams and the Gardiners.

Fitzwilliam Darcy

The hero of the novel is more difficult for the reader to interpret than its heroine. This is because Austen gives her authorial point of view to help us judge Elizabeth far more frequently than she does for Darcy.

Almost all we learn of him at the outset is through the eyes and judgements of other people. These judgements are full of contradictions which readers have to find their own way through. He is introduced in a social setting, at the public ball in Meryton with all the qualities of a hero.

Insufferably proud?

However, Darcy's first act is to reject the company of the locals, which immediately makes him a source of annoyance for more of the characters than Elizabeth, whose first impression of him is of his pride: he hurts her feelings by refusing to dance with her (for a full discussion of pride see pp. 51–52 in 'Themes'). Austen's authorial voice sums up Elizabeth's thoughts about the Bingleys, but on Darcy, she gives the judgement passed by all the characters at the ball:

> …he was looked at with great admiration for about half the evening, till his manners gave a disgust which turned the tide of his popularity; for he was discovered to be proud; to be above his company, and above being pleased…

(Ch. 3, p. 10)

From a thoughtful reader's point of view, this may not entirely be interpreted as snobbery: he has a right to be reserved in a difficult situation, as Charlotte Lucas later points out, but not to make the ungentlemanly remark that upsets Elizabeth.

Austen soon makes it obvious that Darcy has noticed Elizabeth and finds her attractive, but Elizabeth continues to judge him harshly because of the initial rejection. Conversation between the two during Elizabeth's stay at Netherfield shows them to be worthy opponents in cut-and-thrust exchanges of views.

Darcy does not act on his growing feelings, having been exposed to the behaviour of her mother and sisters, particularly at a more formal social gathering, the Netherfield ball. This is an important turning point in the novel, as the uncouth behaviour of the Bennet family convinces him he needs to separate Bingley from Jane. It also accentuates the social gulf between him and Elizabeth.

By comparison with Bingley, Darcy is initially presented as mean-spirited, though his positive qualities are also developed. From his behaviour throughout the novel, it is made clear that Darcy is a close friend of

---

Key quotation

…his friend Mr. Darcy soon drew the attention of the room by his fine, tall person, handsome features, noble mien; and the report which was in general circulation within five minutes after his entrance, of his having ten thousand a year. The gentlemen pronounced him to be a fine figure of a man, the ladies declared he was much handsomer than Mr. Bingley, and he was looked at with great admiration…

(Ch. 3, p. 10)

Build critical skills

Why does Austen rarely let her reader share Darcy's point of view? Is it mainly so we empathise more with the heroine? Or so that Darcy's good points are withheld so we, like Elizabeth, develop a prejudice against him?

Bingley, which demonstrates his lack of snobbery — Bingley does not come from a landed family; he rents Netherfield. As the plot progresses, Austen shows us how Darcy guides his friend in the ways of living as a gentleman, looking out for his interests with loyalty and selflessness.

For this reason, Darcy's interference in the developing affection between Bingley and Jane enables the reader to understand that he is protecting his friend from hurt. From Elizabeth's initial point of view, however, it looks like cruelty. Austen shows us the irony of how, even though Darcy succeeds in keeping his easy-going friend away from the danger of an unsuitable match, he is unable to save himself from the same fate. We see how his feelings overwhelm his judgement (it is easy to believe that Darcy has never felt so strongly for anyone) when he proposes to Elizabeth (see 'Plot and structure', p. 22). The reader is invited to share Elizabeth's judgement of his words as ill-mannered, patronising and proudly self-assured. Darcy is taken aback by her refusal, presented as considering himself way beyond the expectations of a girl of Elizabeth's social standing.

Able to admit he was wrong

Elizabeth's rejection becomes a turning point for Darcy. Her words, especially the accusation that he has not behaved as a gentleman, disturb him greatly. The letter of explanation he writes almost immediately is Austen's means of giving the reader a first real insight into Darcy's motivation (see 'Plot and structure', pp. 22–23). Here he is presented as at pains to gain Elizabeth's good opinion, explaining in detail why he thought it best to remove Bingley from Netherfield and exactly what Wickham had done to lose his favour. The letter includes private information about his sister that could damage his family's reputation if Elizabeth makes it public. Thus Austen presents to the reader evidence of his integrity, his concern for others close to him and his trust of Elizabeth.

The reader's attitude softens, understanding what it must have cost Darcy to write of such experiences. It takes Elizabeth a little more time to reflect on the content, but eventually we see how she moves from total disbelief to a new understanding of both Darcy and herself.

A liberal gentleman

At Pemberley the true Darcy is finally revealed (see 'Plot and structure', pp. 23–24): the honest comments of his housekeeper and the reflection of the man given by his house and estate complete the reversal of Elizabeth's judgement of him and confirm for the reader what he or she has suspected from the start.

Build critical skills

Characters are constructed by the author. At this point in the story, find some examples of where information about Darcy has earlier been withheld. How does this letter cause the reader to reconsider their first impressions of him?

Key quotation

'He is the best landlord and the best master... not like the wild young men now-a-days who think of nothing but themselves. There is not one of his tenants or servants but what will give him a good name. Some people call him proud, but I never saw anything of it...it is only because he does not rattle away like other young men.'

Mrs Reynolds of Mr Darcy (Ch. 43, pp. 190–91)

Darcy's treatment of the Gardiners is now all civility, despite their social inferiority. Austen shows us that his disdain of other members of the Bennet family was grounded on judgement rather than snobbery. Later generous actions, when Lydia elopes, cement Elizabeth's love for him. His second proposal is followed by a conversation which presents Darcy's journey towards self-knowledge (see 'Plot and structure', p. 26). Her good influence on him continues into their marriage: at the end of the novel we see she was right that Darcy's tolerance and social ease is greatly enhanced by her teasing and 'sportive manner'.

Key quotation

...by her ease and liveliness, his mind might have been softened, his manners improved...
(Ch. 50, p. 239)

Jane Bennet

Jane, the eldest Bennet sister, is recognised as the neighbourhood beauty. She is more conventionally attractive (fair to Elizabeth's dark colouring), more compliant and less challenging than her sister and therefore at first presented as more like the 'heroine', as these are qualities that men, stereotypically, are assumed to value. Jane is both an obvious contrast with her sister and, at times, a means of emphasising either Elizabeth's virtues or her failings.

▲ Jane (left) with Elizabeth in the 2005 film

Key quotation

'You never see a fault in any body. All the world are good and agreeable in your eyes. I never heard you speak ill of a human being in my life.'

Elizabeth of Jane (Ch. 4, p. 14)

Key quotation

'This will not do,' said Elizabeth. 'You never will be able to make both of them good for anything. Take your choice, but you must be satisfied with only one. There is but such a quantity of merit between them; just enough to make one good sort of man....'

Speaking to Jane of Wickham and Darcy (Ch. 40, p. 174)

Key quotation

'You are each of you so complying, that nothing will ever be resolved on; so easy, that every servant will cheat you; and so generous, that you will always exceed your income.'

Mr Bennet on Jane and Bingley (Ch. 55, p. 268)

We are introduced to Jane by her mother's conversation (Elizabeth is '...not half so handsome as Jane...', Ch. 1, p. 6). The Bennets are all presented as having their own opinions about their new neighbour, but the first time Jane contributes to any conversation is after she has caught Bingley's eye and danced with him at the Meryton ball. She is presented as less willing to be censorious of their new neighbours than her sister. The reader has to concur with Caroline Bingley's judgement of her as 'a sweet girl' (Ch. 4, p. 16).

In social situations Jane says little: she accepts invitations to dance, she smiles and makes herself pleasant company and she wins affection from all, unlike her more opinionated sister. She is befriended by Caroline Bingley and becomes a welcome visitor at Netherfield. When she takes to bed with a cold, little is heard of her although the Bingleys take care of her and Mr Bingley does not want her to leave.

Jane's intimate conversations with Elizabeth serve the purpose of providing a moderating influence on Elizabeth's judgements, for Jane always sees the best in anybody or any situation. The reader sees how:

- She defends Darcy against accusations of being disagreeable (Ch. 5).
- She wishes Charlotte happiness in her marriage with Collins (Ch. 24).
- At different times in the novel, she defends Darcy against Wickham's accusation of bad treatment (Ch. 17), then defends Wickham when the situation is reversed (Ch. 40).

At times Jane is naïve, but she is not presented as a weak character. When her hopes of Bingley are dashed by his sudden departure, Jane's ability to suffer in silence becomes her most obvious characteristic. In fact, her capacity for concealing strong feelings turns out to lie at the root of Darcy's doubts of her affection for Bingley. Austen shows the reader that, over months, it is Jane's way of coping with separation. She says little, except to Elizabeth, despite her mother's constant talk of his leaving. We see how she writes to Caroline, refusing to believe that she had anything to do with Bingley's change of heart. Even when Jane stays in London and is rudely ignored by the Bingley sisters, she refuses to see any bad in them and finds reasons for their failure to call on her. The most condemnation she ever shows is in the letter she sends to Elizabeth (Ch. 26, pp. 116–17) and even there, we see how she talks of feeling 'pity' and not wishing to 'judge harshly'.

Her reward for her goodness is the love of the man she has waited for. Once Darcy is assured that her affection is real, Bingley is encouraged to pursue his suit and they are happily engaged, though Austen creates humour from Mr Bennet's cynical insight into his daughter's gentle and generous character as he gives his blessing to the match.

All of the Bennet sisters serve in some way as contrasts to Elizabeth, either to highlight her qualities as a heroine, or to illuminate her human failings. Your ability to comment on the author's use of characterisation, rather than to discuss characters as if they were real people, will lead to high grade evaluation.

Charles Bingley

First impressions of Bingley make him seem like the hero of the novel. Like Jane to Elizabeth, he serves a double purpose as a contrast and a foil for Darcy. The narrative, famously, begins with a reference to his eligibility as a husband when his plans to rent Netherfield become known. Bingley's good looks and sociability make him a favourite at his first social gathering at the Meryton ball. He dances every dance and promises to hold a ball in his new home. He is explicitly contrasted with Darcy as having none of his intolerance of others.

In conversation he is shown to be pleasant and, like Jane, inclined to see the good in everyone. Austen indicates that his attraction to her is also immediate: she is 'the most beautiful creature I ever beheld!' (Ch. 3, p. 11).

Bingley is rich (£5,000 a year) but his social status is not as great as Darcy's. His father, we learn, made money through trade, enough to buy his children an entrance into society. However, they do not have the background of property and land ownership of the traditional upper classes, here represented by Darcy's family. They are what we might now call *nouveau riche*. Darcy is presented as guiding his friend in the ways of living as a gentleman.

Just as Jane serves a purpose as a contrast with Elizabeth, so Bingley serves a purpose as a contrast to Darcy. Once again, your ability to comment on the author's use of characterisation, rather than simply discussing characters as if they were real people, will lead to top-grade evaluation.

Bingley's lack of snobbery and simple goodness is demonstrated as he openly shows his preference for Jane's company. When she becomes ill at Netherfield he is most concerned for her welfare. Elizabeth's arrival there gives more opportunities to study him in conversation with Darcy. Like

Key quotation

'Arguments are too much like disputes. If you and Miss Bennet will defer yours till I am out of the room, I shall be very thankful....'
Bingley to Darcy (Ch. 10, p. 42)

Elizabeth, he admits to being easily influenced and to disliking arguments. We can also judge him as not being clever enough to take part in, or even enjoy, the verbal sparring of Darcy and Elizabeth. We also see him admit to not being much of a reader or a writer of letters, unlike Darcy.

Bingley says he is impulsive, and his leaving for London so soon after the Netherfield ball reflects this. It is only later that the reader, through Elizabeth, discovers that Darcy has persuaded him that Jane is not the one for him, not simply because of her unsuitable family, which would hardly bother Bingley, but because she has no real feelings for him. This aspect of his behaviour reflects Bingley's compliant nature.

When Bingley discovers Jane's stay in London was concealed from him, the reader is shown that he has the spirit to be angry, but he is not a man to bear a grudge. He returns to Netherfield and resumes his courting, charming even the sarcastic Mr Bennet. Darcy watches and, once convinced that Jane returns Bingley's love, gives his approval to the ever-compliant Bingley, prompting the proposal in Ch. 55.

Austen shows that, as a couple, Bingley and Jane suit each other well. However, she also summarises in Ch. 61 that they have much to be grateful for in the continued love and guidance they will receive from Darcy and Elizabeth, for they do not possess the Darcys' capacity for mutual improvement.

The other Bennet sisters

GRADE *BOOSTER*

The younger three daughters are less rounded as characters. They are also presented as a contrast to Elizabeth, almost as caricatures of female failings. Your ability to comment on how Austen exaggerates characters like these for humorous effect will gain you marks if you are asked to write about any of the less central characters in the novel.

Mary

Third sister in terms of age, she is a parody of the idea of an 'accomplished' woman. She is plain and has compensated by bettering herself. Austen has her cynical father introduce her in conversation: 'you are a young lady of deep reflection...and read great books and make extracts' (Ch. 2, p. 8). Mary's opinions frequently sound pompous and give the impression that they derive more from her reading than any understanding of the world. Her character is a contrast with Elizabeth's, whose comments reflect a sharp intellect and perceptive understanding of the people around her.

Mary is frequently absent from the social occasions that occupy her sisters' time, preferring to read. However, there is one occasion where her actions contribute to Elizabeth's embarrassment about her family: the Netherfield ball. Despite Elizabeth's best attempts to deter her, Mary accepts an invitation to sing to the assembled guests. Elizabeth's 'agonies' are shared with the reader through authorial comment: 'Mary's powers were by no means fitted to such a display; her voice was weak and her manner affected' (Ch. 18, p. 81). At the same time as empathising with Elizabeth, the reader is invited to find amusement in Mary's vanity and affectation as might others in the room, such as Caroline Bingley. Elizabeth's embarrassment, and the reader's amusement, is compounded when Mr Bennet brings the recital to a halt in a sarcastic way, saying: 'You have delighted us long enough' (Ch. 18, p. 81). Mary then slips back into the shadows until the close of the novel where we learn that she benefits from the absence of her sisters as this requires her to spend more of her time socialising with her mother and less time reading and reflecting.

Catherine (Kitty) and Lydia

The younger daughters are almost indistinguishable for the first half of the novel. They are, as their father describes them, 'silly and ignorant' (p. 6), presented as stereotypes at the opposite end of the spectrum from Mary: empty-headed girls, obsessed with shopping, clothes, parties, gossip and flirting with young men. They are also shown to be their mother's daughters and on many occasions she encourages their frivolous behaviour, reminiscing about her own youthful behaviour: 'I cried for two day's altogether when Colonel Miller's regiment went away', and indulging their extravagant spending on clothes. They are uneducated, sometimes vulgar and often presented as a source of shame to Elizabeth.

Lydia is brought to the fore when Jane and Elizabeth return from Hunsford. She and Kitty have been allowed to bring the family carriage, unaccompanied, to meet their sisters en route back from London.

Lydia's conversation, in this chapter as elsewhere, is unendingly about the officers, particularly Wickham. She becomes a means for Austen to demonstrate how inadequate the Bennets have been as parents. Still not quite 16, Lydia wishes to follow the regiment to Brighton and her mother encourages her — indeed she would like to go with her. Despite Elizabeth's warnings about possible dangers, her father also fails to act responsibly, presented here as almost not caring what consequences could follow: '...she cannot grow many degrees worse without authorising us to lock her up for the rest of her life' (Ch. 41, p. 180).

Build critical skills

Reread the conversation in Ch. 39, p. 170–71. The extent of the girls' purchases is almost slapstick comedy as they struggle to fit everything into the coach. Consider how amusement for the reader is created as Lydia's thoughtless extravagance is exaggerated.

Key quotation

'I have bought this bonnet. I do not think it is very pretty; but I thought I might as well buy it as not. I shall pull it to pieces as soon as I get home, and see if I can make it up any better.'

Lydia on shopping (Ch. 39, p. 170)

The worst does happen: Lydia's flirtations end in elopement with Wickham. This could have destroyed the Bennet family's reputation and any hopes of good marriages for her sisters. Lydia, however, shows by her conversation and her actions that she has no shame: she shows off her wedding ring to passing acquaintances, recommends that her sisters follow her example of finding husbands in Brighton, and flaunts her feckless husband and married status. She is summed up by Austen's authorial comment as 'untamed, unabashed, wild, noisy and fearless' (Ch. 51, p. 241).

Mr and Mrs Bennet

Many writers in the eighteenth century adhered to the convention of creating paired characters to serve a range of purposes — some characters would be very similar (like the Bingley 'ugly sisters') and others would be complete opposites. These pairings help the reader to form judgements about characters. The Bennets are presented to us as an ill-matched couple and the faults of each are exaggerated for humorous effect.

Mr Bennet

In Mr Bennet, Austen creates a believable character, presenting him as clever but made cynical by the disappointments of an unfortunate marriage. The reader learns that he married a pretty but silly woman, who was beneath his social station, and now regrets the decision. For this reason, he makes an important contribution to the theme of marriage (see 'Themes' section, pp. 45–48).

Mr Bennet is caricatured as a neglectful father, spending most of his time hidden away from his family of women in the peace of his library. Austen's skill in constructing his cynical commentary on events is a source of great amusement for the reader, particularly when he comments ironically on foolish characters like Mr Collins.

He is shown to be respectful of his two elder daughters, especially Elizabeth who shares his incisive wit. Towards his younger daughters, however, he has simply been negligent, leaving them to their mother and finding their foolishness either a source of irritation or amusement. On several occasions Austen shows him to reflect on his failure to act as he should have done as a wise spouse and father, most notably after Lydia's elopement. In this he also contributes to the theme of parenthood (see 'Themes' section, pp. 48–50). However, as a two-dimensional character, he is not going to change. His final remark about admiring all his sons-in-law, though 'Wickham, perhaps, is my favourite' (Ch. 59, p. 292), shows he is still the detached, cynical observer of fools that he was at the start of the novel.

Key quotation

'An unhappy alternative is before you, Elizabeth. From this day forward you must be a stranger to one of your parents. Your mother will never see you again if you do not marry Mr Collins, and I will never see you again if you do.'

(Ch. 20, p. 90)

Mrs Bennet

Austen presents Mrs Bennet as a caricature of a woman of little understanding and inferior background. She is shown to be as superficial, frivolous and extravagant as her younger daughters. In her youth she is said to have had good looks and good humour, like her daughter Lydia. These qualities have both faded. Her failure to be a good wife has been compounded by failure to produce a son to inherit the estate, and in this respect maybe the reader is invited to feel some pity for her, though mainly we see a stereotypical mother of daughters, with little else to occupy her mind than the wish to see her daughters married and independent of the consequences of entailment. In this, like Mr Bennet, she too contributes to the themes of marriage and parenthood (see pp. 45–50).

Like her husband, she is a source of humour, but in a different way, for her conversation caricatures 'ill-breeding': she speaks too loudly and of the most inappropriate things, or nonsensical things, contradicting herself from one sentence to the next. The reader witnesses (and smiles at) the embarrassment she causes her daughters in company, notably at the Netherfield ball, where her loud comments about Jane's hopes of marrying Bingley cause Darcy to remove him. She is shown to be as selfish as a child and, when things do not go the way she wants, she falls ill with 'nerves'.

Her husband takes delight in mocking her, adding to the couple's humorous contribution to the novel. Her failings and 'low connections' are, ironically, the biggest obstacle to what she most wants: marriage for her daughters.

Elizabeth's other suitors

> **GRADE BOOSTER**
>
> All romantic novels include a love rival (or two) for the heroine's affections. These rivals turn out to be unsuitable as husbands for a range of reasons. Showing an understanding of aspects of the genre in your response by referring to this kind of detail should gain marks.

Mr Collins

Mr Collins is a truly comic character, a fool made almost **grotesque** by exaggeration. The presentation of his character goes beyond caricature to satire. He is the nearest male relative to Mr Bennet and thus the heir to Longbourn. From the moment he introduces himself in his letter to Mr Bennet, he is a strange mix of pompous self-importance (in this he has some similarity to Mary) and cringing deference to his social superiors. His obsequious admiration of Lady Catherine and all she does makes him blind to what she really is: an overbearing busybody.

Key quotation

'*...you must not expect such girls to have the sense of their father and mother. — When they get to our age, I dare say they will not think about officers any more than we do. I remember the time when I liked a red coat myself very well — and indeed so I do still at my heart....*'
(Ch. 7, p. 25)

Key quotation

'*...a woman of mean understanding, little information, and uncertain temper....*'
Austen's authorial comment sums up Mrs Bennet with a triple (Ch. 1, p. 7)

grotesque: strange, absurd, ridiculous — often in a way which is unexpected and disturbing

He is presented as totally lacking in self-knowledge and any kind of self-awareness, which leads him to behave in a manner which is embarrassing to those around him, but of which he is totally oblivious. This is a source of entertainment for Mr Bennet and, of course, the reader.

When we read his proposal to Elizabeth, we can see how Austen portrays him as devoid of any empathy or understanding of any other point of view from his own. He is hurt when Elizabeth refuses him as he is unable to comprehend what he has done to deserve rejection. His feelings seem to have limited intensity as he moves almost immediately on to Charlotte Lucas, betraying no awareness at all of how absurd this makes him look.

▲ Mr Collins with Elizabeth in the 2005 film

Once home with his new bride, the quality he most exhibits is materialism, in his attitude to his own 'humble abode' and even more so when he has the opportunity to show off the superficial splendours of Lady Catherine's property. His admiration of cost and quantity disclose a complete lack of taste or discernment.

Key quotation

'...she [Lady Catherine] said, 'Mr. Collins, you must marry. A clergyman like you must marry. — Chuse properly, chuse a gentlewoman for my sake; and for your own, let her be an active useful sort of person, not brought up high, but able to make a small income go a good way.'

Part of Mr Collins' proposal of marriage to Elizabeth (Ch. 19, p. 85)

Key quotation

Mr Collins was not a sensible man...altogether a mixture of pride and obsequiousness, self-importance and humility.

Austen's ironic authorial comment makes use of antithesis to sum up Collins' character (Ch. 15, p. 57)

Build critical skills

The irony of Mr Collins is that, as a clergyman, he should be humble, tolerant, forgiving, generous, spiritual, but he shows himself again and again to be the opposite. Read the letter on the final page of Ch. 57, p. 280 beginning 'I am truly rejoiced that my cousin Lydia's sad business...'. How does this extremely unforgiving condemnation of Lydia's behaviour reveal his character?

Mr George Wickham

Mr George Wickham's characterisation is a contrast with that of Mr Collins. He is not a comic suitor. At first Austen appears to present him as competition for Darcy. He is good-looking, charming, easy company as he singles out Elizabeth for his attentions, taking her into his confidence with the story of how Darcy denied him the promise of a career in the church.

Mrs Gardiner observes the two of them together and warns Elizabeth not to become too involved with Wickham, although her warning is about his financial status rather than any fault of character. Her caution is later justified, however, because the next we hear of Wickham is that he has transferred his interest to a rich heiress, Miss King.

Austen gradually allows the reader access to the truth. Elizabeth criticises Darcy's treatment of Wickham when she rejects his proposal. Darcy's response is to reveal the reasons Wickham lost the promised inheritance: he chose 'a life of idleness and dissipation' (Ch. 35, p. 157) rather than a career in the church; he wasted the money Darcy gave him instead of the promised living, and failed in his second choice of employment, law; shockingly (and with an element of forewarning) he then attempted to elope with 15-year-old Georgiana Darcy to get his hands on her fortune.

The plot then reveals how, thwarted in that attempt, Wickham tries his hand at a military career, which comes to a dishonourable conclusion when he succeeds in eloping with Lydia, leaving behind him a muddle of unpaid gambling debts both in Meryton and Brighton.

Minor characters

Any novel as long and complex as *Pride and Prejudice* will include a variety of minor and less rounded characters who may contribute to development of plot or themes, or may just serve as contrasts to the main characters in the text.

Colonel Fitzwilliam

Although he only appears in the book for eight chapters, Colonel Fitzwilliam is important as a third love rival for the hero.

He is Darcy's cousin, and is presented as a total contrast to him: agreeable company, intelligent, polite and an entertaining conversationalist. One function he serves is to show Elizabeth's liveliness and humour to best advantage in front of his quieter cousin.

He contributes to the development of the theme of money and marriage: he is a younger son of a lord, Darcy's mother's brother, and is thus an aristocrat like Lady Catherine, but as he has no hope of inheriting a fortune, he will have to ensure that he considers money when choosing a wife (Ch. 33, p. 143). With unfortunate timing, just before Darcy proposes

---

Build critical skills

Wickham is not a comic character: he is a villain against whom the hero may be judged. Make a list of Darcy's virtues, such as his morally unimpeachable character, his honesty, his loyalty, his integrity and, for each, identify evidence of George Wickham's behaviour which show him to be the complete opposite.

Build critical skills

Remind yourself of Colonel Fitzwilliam's first appearance in the novel (end of Ch. 30 p. 133 to Ch. 31, p. 137). What do we learn about Fitzwilliam? Why does Austen introduce him at this point in the plot?

marriage to Elizabeth he reveals to her that Darcy saved his friend Bingley from 'the inconveniences of a most imprudent marriage' (Ch. 33, p. 145).

Mrs Bennet's family

Mrs Philips

Mrs Philips is very like her sister: shallow, frivolous, extravagant and unable to conduct herself properly in polite society. Fond of company and gossip, she shows little awareness of propriety and is one of the Bennet family connections Darcy finds 'objectionable'. She is less a source of humour than of amazed embarrassment from any reader who has empathy with Elizabeth's feelings.

Mr and Mrs Gardiner

Mrs Bennet's brother is a total contrast to her: he and his wife are presented as rounded characters, educated and cultured. Their intelligence and manners are evident despite their lower social class. They are first mentioned, and snobbishly dismissed, by Caroline Bingley as living 'somewhere near Cheapside', an allusion to Mr Gardiner's employment in 'trade' (Ch. 8, p. 30).

Mrs Gardiner is presented as a contrast to both her husband's sisters, with an intellect which matches his, good manners and good sense 'an amiable, intelligent, elegant woman' (a triple in Austen's authorial voice, p. 110). We grow to know her better than her husband as Austen describes how she supports Jane after her disappointment with Bingley and spends time with Elizabeth, warning her to be wary of a relationship with Wickham, then offering the distraction of a trip to the north of England when that relationship comes to nothing. Mrs Gardiner grew up in Derbyshire so suggests visiting Pemberley where they are made welcome by Darcy and conduct themselves faultlessly.

They contribute to the theme of parenthood and family relationships. (See 'Themes', p. 49.)

The Bingley sisters

Miss Caroline Bingley and Mrs Louisa Hurst provide a double act of stereotypical female behaviour — pantomime 'ugly sisters' to Elizabeth's Cinderella. They are presented as untrustworthy, ill-mannered snobs. They are also ill-educated and rather stupid.

Georgiana Darcy

By contrast with the Bingley sisters, Georgiana is a real lady. She reflects positively on her brother to whom she owes gratitude. She is contrasted

> **GRADE BOOSTER**
>
> By contrast in their behaviour, the Bingley sisters serve to emphasise Elizabeth and Jane's positive qualities. Although they are ladies of fashion and position, they are dislikeable characters. Commenting on such contrasts will help to boost your grade.

with Lydia, sharing the experience of being ensnared by Wickham, but saved by a caring, competent family, unlike the ineffective Bennets. She is shown as requiring the guidance both of her older brother and his chosen wife, who she grows to love and respect.

Charlotte Lucas

Charlotte is an intimate friend of Elizabeth's, intelligent, sensible and, at 27 years old, mature and level-headed. She loses some of the reader's sympathy when she marries the ridiculous Mr Collins. However, she justifies her decision with reasonable arguments about her expectations: rather than being 'an old maid' and a financial burden on her brothers, she takes what comfort she can from a loveless marriage. Her contribution to the theme of marriage is further discussed in 'Themes' on p. 46.

Lady Catherine de Bourgh and her daughter, Anne

Lady Catherine is another great comic creation. With rank and status superior to most other characters, she has an exaggerated certainty of her own importance. Mr Collins' awe of her superiority is a further source of humour.

Lady Catherine (the sister of Darcy's mother) plays an important role in advancing the plot when she instructs Elizabeth not to marry Darcy (Ch. 56), ironically leading Elizabeth to wonder whether such a proposal might happen, and to dismiss her arguments. Anne is the heiress to Rosings and her mother hopes she will marry her cousin, Darcy. Anne could not be more of a contrast to Lady Catherine, with nothing to say for herself at all. Her function is to be the peg on which her mother's fantasies and dreams are hung. Elizabeth describes her as 'sickly and cross' (p. 125.)

Lady Catherine's estate at Rosings satirises a fashion for modernising and 'improving' great houses, a contrast with the real beauty of Pemberley (see discussion on p. 66).

Build critical skills

The rise of the moneyed middle classes into the nobility was an aspect of eighteenth-century social change. Austen reinforces some conventional stereotypes, e.g. the Bingley sisters' lack of manners and Lady Catherine's expensively furnished home and stiffly formal lifestyle. Can you think of other examples?

However, Austen is revolutionary in depicting the blurring of class distinctions, e.g. in Darcy's marriage to Elizabeth and the friendship between the Darcys and the Gardiners. Identify other characters who move comfortably in a class superior to their own by virtue of education.

GRADE *FOCUS*

Grade 5

Students will be aware of characters as having clear purposes in a text. They will select evidence from the text and discuss relevant supporting detail. Their comments on language and structure will be clear and relevant. Discussion of presentation of character will be clear and precise and may begin to consider alternative interpretations.

Grade 8

Students will offer a more perceptive response to hidden meanings and show an ability to grasp irony and to explore alternative readings. Their comments on language and structure will include perceptive analysis. Characters will be seen to represent themes and ideas as well as being believable creations. Discussion of evidence will be more detailed and demonstrate analytical qualities.

REVIEW YOUR LEARNING

(Answers are given on pages 110–111.)

1   What are the main ways Jane Austen presents characters to readers of the novel?

2   What are the names of the three younger Bennet sisters, and what main purpose do they have in the novel?

3   Name two characters who are exaggerated caricatures, and explain their impact on the reader.

4   Which characters do the following phrases describe?
     - 'a sweet girl'
     - 'fine, tall person, handsome features, noble mien'
     - 'untamed, unabashed, wild, noisy and fearless'
     - 'sickly and cross'

5   Who makes the following statements and to whom? What in your opinion does each statement reveal about the speaker?
     - 'You will have a very charming mother-in-law....'
     - 'You have delighted us long enough.'

6   Who makes this comment near the end of the novel: '...how rich and great you will be! What pin money, what jewels, what carriages you will have'?

Themes

Target your thinking

- What is a theme? (**AO1, AO2, AO3**)
- What are the main themes in *Pride and Prejudice*? (**AO1, AO2, AO3**)

A theme in a novel is an idea or group of ideas that the author explores. There is no absolutely correct way to define the themes in a novel, and in any interpretation of literary themes there is bound to be some overlap. Here is a suggested list of themes in *Pride and Prejudice*:

- money and marriage
- parenthood and family relationships
- love and friendship
- pride and prejudice
- appearance and reality

In common with the essayists of the eighteenth century, Austen's novels have a **didactic** purpose: her themes explore issues of morality and judgement, with many chapters beginning and ending with reflection on good and bad, success and failure (see also 'Context' on p. 15).

didactic: intended to teach, particularly a moral lesson

Money and marriage

Pride and Prejudice begins with one of the most famous opening sentences of any novel:

'It is a truth universally acknowledged, that a single man in possession of a good fortune must be in want of a wife.'

The unbreakable link between money and marriage is established right at the beginning. In the context of the novel, love alone cannot be a solid basis for any middle- or upper-class marriage. The fortunes of each of the couples would always have to be an early consideration.

In the book Austen shows four weddings where money plays contrasting levels of importance in making the marriage — those of:

- the Collins
- the Wickhams
- the Bingleys
- the Darcys

Build critical skills

Throughout *Pride and Prejudice* you will notice the witty, mocking tone of the opening statement of the novel as a feature of Austen's style. Can you identify other examples — and relate them to the themes she explores?

45

Key quotation

'I am not romantic, you know. I never was. I ask only a comfortable home; and considering Mr. Collins's character, connections, and situation in life, I am convinced that my chance of happiness with him is as fair as most people can boast on entering the marriage state.'

Charlotte defends her choice to Elizabeth (Ch. 22, pp. 100–101)

The Collins

The first marriage is that of Charlotte Lucas to Collins. She marries for financial security. As well as his comfortable living as a clergyman, he will one day inherit Mr Bennet's estate at Longbourn. At her advanced age of 27, this could well be the only proposal she will ever receive. Charlotte has no personal fortune, but, being the daughter of a knight, is a good enough social catch for Collins, who is a snob.

There are two things Austen invites the reader to consider: Charlotte does not seem to expect the relationship of marriage to make her happy, though her status as a married woman, her own home, and the promise of motherhood and a family life attract her. Also, what does her decision to accept Mr Collins say about concern for her 'best' friend Elizabeth, whose cast-off suitor she accepts, and whose home will one day become hers? Austen suggests that, in the long term, Charlotte's happiness can only be partial. She is an intelligent woman, who certainly has little hope of joy from the company of her foolish husband. Note the use of a triple in Charlotte's description of her husband (see key quotation). This reflects her intelligence and the measured rationality of her approach to marriage.

GRADE *BOOSTER*

```
Proposals of marriage contribute to the structure of
the novel — a refusal, or a disappointment, followed
by acceptance is often the pattern. Here Elizabeth
refused then Charlotte accepted. Where else do you
see similar events? Commenting on aspects of structure
will raise your grade.
```

The Wickhams

Second, Wickham and Lydia marry. Their approach to marriage is a complete contrast to Charlotte's. There is no prudence or weighing up of pros and cons: caught up in their physical attraction to each other, they elope to London causing family scandal. This is the closest Austen comes to relating marriage to sex. Only family interference makes things right for this marriage. First Darcy and then Lydia's uncle intervene (Ch. 52). In effect they pay Wickham to marry Lydia, ensuring a respectable outcome to the relationship.

In the long term, this marriage too will end unhappily. The poor role model of Lydia's parents shows how marriage based on physical attraction, where the couple have very little in common and where their educational levels are so ill-matched, will end with little joy in companionship once their youth and looks have gone.

Austen hints at a level of resentment too: Wickham hoped to make his fortune through a financially advantageous marriage. He tried for Georgiana Darcy and then Miss King. He will be a poor husband, in both senses of the word: hopeless with money and a womaniser as well. Poor Lydia.

The Bingleys

Jane and Bingley have more hopes of a successful future because, in their marriage, Austen presents a balance between the extremes: they are physically attracted; they take genuine pleasure from each other's company; they are alike in many ways — easy-going and not particularly clever. They also have the financial security of Bingley's £5,000 a year. This promises to be a marriage offering each partner good companionship, even if the outlook seems less than ideal to cynical Mr Bennet (see p. 34).

Both money and property indicated the status of men. Bingley's income is good, but he has no property as his father made his fortune fairly recently. Darcy has twice the income and a 'large estate in Derbyshire'. Many people then lived on a wage of between £1 and £2 a week: even Bingley is therefore a millionaire by today's standards. The suggestion that these young men are 'in want of a wife' is ironic, but they are certainly very eligible marriage material.

The Darcys

Finally there is the ideal match. Austen presents to us a marriage that will last, based on love, respect and lengthy consideration rather than short-lived passion, a relationship that has grown and changed the two partners in ways that make them even more compatible and better suited.

Darcy and Elizabeth have it all: he is attracted to her almost from the start and she grows to feel the same attraction to him. However, there is more substance to this relationship: by virtue of education, they are alike in their interests, tastes and views. They have learnt important lessons about how they relate to others, and are likely to go on doing so. Not only are they good for each other, but also for those around them. For example:

> 'Kitty…spent the chief of her time with her two elder sisters… In society so superior to what she had generally known, her improvement was great…she became…less irritable, less ignorant and less insipid.'

(Ch. 61, p. 297)

Finally, Darcy is the richest man of the four, so Elizabeth also gains the security of money and a fine house. There remains the downside of

Key quotation

…such an income as theirs, under the direction of two persons so extravagant in their wants, and heedless of their future, must be very insufficient to their support….

Elizabeth's thoughts on the Wickham's future (Ch. 61, p. 298)

Build critical skills

Read p. 268 in Ch. 55. Remind yourself of the opening of the novel as you consider the conversation where newly engaged Jane talks to her parents about prospects in this marriage. What is Austen suggesting about contemporary attitudes to marriage, and how the Bennets' attitudes contrast?

her embarrassing relatives, but he also has an annoying aunt. However, these burdens are lessened by the provision of a role model for a happy marriage in Elizabeth's Aunt and Uncle Gardiner.

Build critical skills

Austen rarely mentions romantic love in connection with marriage — if anything, passion is a subject of suspicion. Mrs Gardiner and Elizabeth discuss the phrase 'violently in love' (Ch. 25, p. 111). How far do you agree with Mrs Gardiner's comments?

Later, Darcy describes his love for Elizabeth as 'ardent' (Ch. 34, p. 147) and Austen uses the phrase 'violently in love' (Ch. 58, p. 282) to sum up his feelings. Is she now suggesting that passion has a part to play in marriage?

Parenthood and family relationships

How well or badly does a marriage impact on the upbringing of children? This is a recurrent question in Austen's writing. Again, she presents the reader with a number of family relationships to consider — those of:

- the Bennets
- the Gardiners
- the Lucases

The Bennets

> **Key quotation**
>
> *Elizabeth...had never felt so strongly as now the disadvantages which must attend the children of so unsuitable a marriage, nor ever been so fully aware of the evils arising from so ill-judged a direction of talents; talents which, rightly used, might at least have preserved the respectability of his daughters...*
>
> Elizabeth's thoughts about her father (Ch. 42, p. 183)

Austen presents Mr and Mrs Bennet's marriage as prompted by the same impulse of attraction as that between Lydia and Wickham. This, we learn, has faded, leaving them little pleasure in their relationship with each other. Mrs Bennet brought some money into the marriage: 'Five thousand pounds was settled by marriage articles on Mrs Bennet and the children' (p. 236). However, Mr Bennet has not been prudent with the family finances. He has failed to save enough to ensure a secure future for his daughters after his death, when the estate goes to Mr Collins.

Build critical skills

Read the opening of Ch. 50, p. 236–37 on Mr Bennet's regrets about his failings as a provider for his family. How does Austen's use of language ('useless', 'too late', 'inconvenience', 'indolence', 'dilatory') highlight his weaknesses, and use of abstract nouns ('duty', 'honour', 'obligation') reinforce the right way to behave?

Despite their less than perfect marriage, as parents, the Bennets are shown to have done quite well in the upbringing of their elder daughters:

Jane is a good person and Elizabeth's intellect and wit have been encouraged. However, the impact of a silly, ill-educated mother and a sarcastic father who has retreated impatiently into his library is clear in the younger three. Kitty and Lydia, encouraged by their mother are also silly, obsessed by hats, dancing and young men, while Mary strives to be accomplished, without her father's guidance or Elizabeth's intelligence.

Austen highlights how a mismatch between the Bennets' education and, in his case, a failure to turn intellect into intelligent action, has undermined their effectiveness as parents. (There is further discussion of the relationship of Mr and Mrs Bennet in 'Characterisation', pp. 38–39.)

The Gardiners

Mrs Bennet's brother presents a contrasting representation of marriage and family life. Mr Gardiner is of a lower social class. However, this family's life is presented as one well worthy of emulation. Their life is comfortable and civilised with visits to the theatre and shopping in the city. As parents, the Gardiners are a success: their 'troop of little boys and girls' (Ch. 27, p. 120) are loved and cared for.

Mrs Gardiner plays the role of a concerned mother to Elizabeth and Jane far better than Mrs Bennet. Mr Gardiner, in turn, takes on the fatherly role that should rightly have been Mr Bennet's, dealing with the consequences of Lydia's elopement. At the end of the novel, this couple become role models for, and welcome guests of, the couple at Pemberley.

The Lucases

The Bennets' neighbours in Longbourn provide another picture of family life. Sir William's background is also in trade and he has been mayor, which led to his receiving a knighthood. He has spent some of his money on Lucas Lodge and there he presides, affecting the manners he has learnt at the court of St James's, hugely impressed by anyone whose status he perceives to be higher than his own. His wife, Lady Lucas, is described as 'not too clever to be a valuable neighbour to Mrs Bennet' (Ch. 5, p. 16). Note the humorous use of litotes here. (For a definition of 'litotes' see 'Language, style and analysis', p. 60.)

They have 'several children' (Ch. 5, p. 16), the oldest being Charlotte who demonstrates cynical views about marriage (see 'Money and marriage' above). There is a younger daughter, Maria, whose awe of her social superiors is shown to be like her father's when they visit the aristocratic Lady Catherine (Ch. 29, pp. 126–27).

One of her younger brothers says: 'If I were as rich as Mr Darcy...I should not care how proud I was. I would keep a pack of foxhounds, and drink a bottle of wine every day' (Ch. 5, p. 18). The Lucas parents are, thus, presented as somewhat limited role models for happy family life.

Key quotation

With the Gardiners they were always on the most intimate terms. Darcy, as well as Elizabeth, really loved them.

(Ch. 61, p. 299)

49

The young couples

Good marriages lead to solid parenting and the reader is invited to speculate about how the quality of the various marriages shown will shape their family life. The Darcys and Bingleys begin to act as parents to Kitty even before they have children of their own. Jane has already had practice with her Gardiner nephews and nieces, 'teaching them, playing with them and loving them' (note this triple of virtuous acts used to emphasise Jane's suitability as a potential mother; Ch. 42, p. 186). Both couples have promise as parents.

The best that can be hoped for the Collins' children is that they will have a sensible loving mother. The insubstantial basis for the Wickhams' marriage holds out little hope for any children.

Love and friendship

Ideally love and friendship are a part of marriage, but not necessarily so, as outlined above. Austen shows that good friendships, like good marriages, lead to the mutual improvement and growth of both parties.

Elizabeth and Jane

Elizabeth and Jane are presented to the reader as friends as well as sisters and Elizabeth's ability to give support and guidance compensates for their inadequate parents. All major events in their lives are shared in person or by letter: for example Jane's disappointment when the Bingleys leave Netherfield, and her hurt feelings when she is slighted by Caroline in London. They talk over Darcy's supposed injury to Wickham's prospects and the truth about why Darcy acted as he did. They share the shame and anxiety Lydia causes and finally take joy from each other's happiness at the conclusion of the novel, though not before Jane has assured herself that Elizabeth is not planning to 'marry without affection' (Ch. 59, p. 288). Jane's benevolence and Elizabeth's intelligence are shown to be a basis for life-long positive impact upon their friendship.

Charlotte and Elizabeth

Charlotte and Elizabeth have a close friendship that continues despite Charlotte's unpromising marriage. She is introduced as being 'a sensible, intelligent young woman' (Ch. 5, p. 16) and there are certainly occasions where her opinions prove to be right in the long term, for example when she advises Elizabeth that Darcy's stand-offish behaviour at the Meryton ball may have been misinterpreted. She also warns her that Jane may be limiting her chances of romance with Bingley by not making her feelings more obvious — the very reason Darcy decides to separate them.

Elizabeth's reservations about Charlotte's marriage to Collins makes her question whether they will ever share confidences in the same way they had been used to. However, they remain friends. Charlotte is the first person to suspect that Darcy might be in love with Elizabeth (Ch. 32) and certainly Elizabeth's sympathy for Charlotte's situation in Hunsford is heartfelt.

Darcy and Bingley

Darcy and Bingley are also presented as having a good friendship: Darcy sees Bingley's faults (much as Elizabeth is aware of Jane's and Charlotte's): his trusting nature (he might not realise that Jane could be a fortune hunter, given the attitude to marriage that seems to be prevalent in Meryton) and his reluctance to argue with or hurt people. Darcy decides to separate Bingley from Jane before any harm is done.

Austen shows through this friendship that Darcy is not a snob: his background and social status are superior to Bingley's (Caroline's lack of manners makes this clear) but this does not hold him back. He and Bingley are shown to have qualities that are mutually beneficial and will go on being so throughout life: like Elizabeth, Bingley helps to soften Darcy's seriousness and to encourage his sociability, whilst Darcy will shape the suggestible Bingley into a country gentleman of his own kind.

Pride and prejudice

As with many of Austen's themes, the idea of opposition and balance is explored. When you first begin to read, it is easy to think this theme is a simple matter of Darcy being too proud (and having to learn not to be) and Elizabeth being prejudiced against him (and having to learn not to be).

> **GRADE BOOSTER**
>
> Everyone judges Darcy to be proud when he rejects dancing partners both at Meryton and Lucas Lodge. As ever, beware of what 'everyone' thinks, as the common view is almost always misguided. A grasp of irony and understanding of the subtext in responses can gain high marks.

It is not so straightforward, however: Darcy is also early on shown to be subject to prejudice when he claims he will rarely revise negative judgements (remember the novel was originally written with the title of *First Impressions*).

Key quotation

'I remember hearing you once say, Mr. Darcy, that you hardly ever forgave, that your resentment once created was unappeasable. You are very cautious, I suppose, as to its *being* created.'

'I am,' said he, with a firm voice.

'And never allow yourself to be blinded by prejudice?'

'I hope not.'

'It is particularly incumbent on those who never change their opinion, to be secure of judging properly at first.'
Elizabeth and Darcy (Ch. 18, pp. 75–76)

Pride

Elizabeth, too, is responding to hurt pride in her rejection of Darcy both at the start of the novel and when he makes his first unwilling and ungracious proposal to her.

Austen offers us an interesting distinction between pride and vanity when Charlotte Lucas speaks sense about Darcy:

> 'His pride…does not offend *me* so much as pride often does, because there is an excuse for it. One cannot wonder that so very fine a young man, with family, fortune, everything in his favour, should think highly of himself. If I may so express it, he has a *right* to be proud.'
>
> (Ch. 5, pp. 17–18)

Mary's contribution to this conversation derives from her reading of Fanny Burney's novel *Cecilia,* published in 1782 (the title *Pride and Prejudice* in fact comes from a sentence in this novel):

> 'Vanity and pride are different things, though the words are often used synonymously. A person may be proud without being vain. Pride relates more to our opinion of ourselves, vanity to what we would have others think of us.'
>
> (Ch. 5, p. 18)

Darcy's superior status gives him reason to be reserved in comparatively humble company. From a thoughtful reader's point of view, as Charlotte reminds us, his 'pride' at Meryton was justified when he finds himself in a room full of unfamiliar people, socially inferior to him, well knowing that many of those present will see him as a 'good catch' for someone's daughter, a girl of a social class he would judge as unequal to his own.

Darcy puts his manners down to shyness later in the book (Ch. 31, p. 137), a quality he is shown to share with his younger sister, but he is prepared to admit he has been guilty of '[thinking] meanly of all the rest of the world…of their sense and worth compared with my own' (Ch. 58, p. 284). He tells Elizabeth that her words as she rejected his first proposal set him on the path to remedying that fault of character.

Prejudice

Austen shows how Elizabeth's hurt pride leads her into trouble, making her an easy catch for Wickham: his stories of mistreatment by Darcy reflect her bad opinion and fuel her dislike. Conversely, Wickham flatters her pride by singling her out and treating her as special. It is only after she learns the truth about him that she realises that prejudice in his favour prevented her from questioning the appropriateness of his easy intimacy upon so slender an acquaintance.

Austen presents us with two events to undo the damage: first, Elizabeth's angry reaction to his proposal provokes Darcy's letter. This goes a long way towards explaining his actions and allows her to reconsider the defects of character she believed him to have (see 'Plot and structure', pp. 22–23, for further discussion), whilst he begins to find self-knowledge through the writing of it.

Secondly, Elizabeth's visit to Pemberley eradicates any lingering feelings of prejudice: seeing Darcy's house explains his discomfort in the parochial world of Meryton, and hearing everyone in his household talk of him with such warmth upends her prejudiced opinions. We see how he, likewise, greets her relations with warmth and civility their social status would not have warranted, with no hint of pride or superiority (see 'Plot and structure', pp. 23–24).

By the time he proposes and she accepts, Austen makes explicit that each has learnt a valuable lesson in tempering pride and overcoming prejudice: judgements will still be made, for they are both thinking rational people, but they will see more clearly and jump to conclusions with less haste in their maturity.

Vanity

There are minor characters in the novel held up for comparison with Darcy who illustrate Mary's point about the difference between pride and vanity:

- Lady Catherine is truly vain, with no real reason. Everything she says shows us her self-centred attitude and conviction that she is always right and always better than everybody else. Compare her unwanted advice to her tenants (Ch. 29, p. 128) with Darcy's genuine concern for their well-being (Ch. 43, pp. 190–91).

- Caroline Bingley is also presented as vain and self-centred. Her snobbery towards Elizabeth and Jane shows her to be less of a genuine lady than she thinks herself.

- Mr Collins is presented as vain in thinking that the reflected glory of Lady Catherine's connection with him makes him better than others. It also makes him pompous, self-centred and stupid to a remarkable degree, contributing to the humour of the novel.

- Lydia's vanity is the fault of character that makes her susceptible to Wickham's flattery and we see how it almost leads to her social downfall.

GRADE **BOOSTER**

If you are asked to write about pride and prejudice, you are likely to gain marks by also writing about those characters other than Elizabeth and Darcy who contribute in a minor way to the presentation of this theme. What could you add about the vanity of Sir William Lucas or the lack of personal pride of Charlotte? What about the small-town prejudices of Mrs Bennet and Mrs Philips?

Appearance and reality

Austen investigates another opposition, linked to the theme of pride and prejudice: how what *appears* to be may be very far from reality. Superficial judgements made by the unthinking crowd are almost always incorrect. The first line in the book makes us ask questions as soon as we start reading: would any single rich young man always need a wife? Why should he? Who would benefit more from the arrangement?

Elizabeth and Darcy both make judgements based on superficial appearance, about each other and about those around them, and it takes months to put things right, as shown in the discussion of their pride and prejudice.

All the Bennet family judge Wickham to be the splendid young man he appears to be and all are let down by him.

The underlying idea of balance

Austen is warning us to be wary of hasty and impulsive behaviour based on emotion rather than reflection. She is arguing against the growing Romantic admiration for spontaneity and emotion (see 'Contexts', p. 12) and shows readers that a middle way, finding a balance between reason and feeling, head and heart, is the best and most sensible option.

GRADE *FOCUS*

Grade 5

Students will be able to identify specific themes and explain in a relevant manner how some characters illustrate aspects of a theme. They will develop a sound personal response and will be able to comment on some aspects of language or context relevant to themes, where tasks offer marks for AO2 and AO3.

Grade 8

Students will be able to sustain discussion about how a range of characters and events illustrate aspects of a theme. They will analyse perceptively the use of language to illustrate the themes and will also consider how the novel can be interpreted in the context of different times in relation to themes, developing a convincing and informed personal opinion.

REVIEW YOUR LEARNING

(Answers are given on page 111.)

1 What is a theme?

2 Which five main themes are identified in this guide?

3 What was Austen's source for the title of this novel, and its major theme?

4 Which marriages illustrate the theme of family life?

5 Who is presented as the main example of the theme of appearance and reality?

6 Why is the theme of marriage related to money rather than love?

7 Do you think the themes are as relevant for a modern reader as they might have been when Austen wrote the novel in the early nineteenth century?

Language, style and analysis

Target your thinking

- What features do the terms 'language' and 'style' refer to? (**AO2**)
- What viewpoints does Jane Austen adopt? (**AO2**)
- How is dialogue used to tell the story? (**AO2**)
- Why are so many letters included in the novel? (**AO1, AO2, AO3**)
- What is significant about Austen's use of description and settings? (**AO1, AO2**)

An author's style, the way language is used, is one of the less obvious features of a novel. So it is a challenge to show how well you understand Austen's style and to demonstrate that you can analyse her use of language in some detail.

GRADE BOOSTER

Most exam tasks give quite a large proportion of marks for comment on language (AO2). As you write, you must show the examiner that your grasp of the novel's language is assured and evaluative in order to reach the high grades.

When you write about style, you show that you understand that the author of a novel has numerous choices. Your job as a literary critic — because that is what you are when you write your exam essay — is to identify what choices Austen has made and to assess how effective they are.

The list below gives some of the main features covered by the terms 'language' and 'style'. Austen has made choices about all of them:

- the **viewpoint** from which the story is told, whether it is third person narrative ('**Elizabeth** passed quietly out of the room' or '**She** turned from the window') or first person narrative ('**I** turned from the window')
- how **techniques** such as exaggeration, caricature, irony and satire add humour to the novel
- how **dialogue** (conversation) is used to advance the narrative and how choices of vocabulary and syntax reveal character
- how **letters** are used to advance the narrative and reveal character
- how **precise choices of vocabulary and syntax** are used in description of people and settings to create specific effects for the reader

Viewpoint

The viewpoint of a novel is the position from which the author tells the story. Some novels are told from a **first person** viewpoint. For example, this story could have been told entirely from Elizabeth Bennet's viewpoint. That would have made a different story as we might have found out more about Elizabeth's view of things, but rather less about other characters in the novel.

Jane Austen tells the story in the **third person**. The author is **narrator** and the characters are referred to by their names, or as 'he/she'. This gives more flexibility, allowing Austen to tell us her views about all characters and events as the plot unfolds, as well as allowing her to move from one character to another and describe how they see events.

GRADE *BOOSTER*

Showing understanding of viewpoint in your exam will help you to reach a higher grade. Two useful terms to understand are:

- the **omniscient narrator** — the story-teller knows everything about everyone in the story and tells the reader the truth
- the **unreliable narrator** — the story is communicated from the viewpoint of a character who may be biased, or know only some of the facts

Austen keeps readers on their toes by moving between the two. Demonstrate to the examiner that you understand *where* she does this and explain *why*.

Although Austen writes in the third person, the viewpoint often allows readers to empathise with Elizabeth. She is the main character and often events are narrated as she sees them. When Elizabeth and Jane visit Lucas Lodge (Ch. 6, pp. 20–22), Austen uses a technique where different viewpoints and perspectives reveal information which is not known to everyone.

She begins by allowing the reader to share a viewpoint not often seen, that of Darcy, giving the reader an insight into his private thoughts. Austen tracks the changes in his feelings about Elizabeth, from openly criticising her looks the first time he sees her, to a realisation that he is attracted to her.

He goes on to describe the experience as 'mortifying' (p. 20):

> ...he was forced to acknowledge her figure to be light and pleasing; and in spite of his asserting that her manners were not those of the fashionable world, he was caught by their easy playfulness.

Key quotation

...no sooner had he made it clear to himself and his friends that she had hardly a good feature in her face, than he began to find it was rendered uncommonly intelligent by the beautiful expression of her dark eyes.

(Ch. 6, p. 20)

No one else knows this, especially not Elizabeth. The paragraph concludes by telling us she was 'perfectly unaware' of this, where Austen is the omniscient narrator.

Austen moves immediately to Elizabeth's opinion of Darcy: 'the man who made himself agreeable nowhere', a biased and unreliable opinion, as Elizabeth's frequently are in the first half of the novel.

An exchange follows (more below about Austen's use of dialogue), then Austen returns to the viewpoint of the omniscient narrator as she compares Elizabeth's singing ('pleasing though by no means capital') with that of her sister Mary, who plays better but gives less pleasure because she 'had neither genius nor taste' (p. 21).

GRADE BOOSTER

Explore the use and effect of the rhetorical devices in Elizabeth's passionate rejection of Darcy's proposal (see 'Top ten moments' no. 5 on p. 104): emotive words, a triple and a rhetorical question. Commenting on the language Austen uses to present her characters will gain you marks.

Build critical skills

How do shifting viewpoints help you to understand more about:
- the character of Jane at the end of Ch. 23, p. 103?
- Lydia in Ch. 41, p. 180?
- reflections on Mr Bennet's failings as a husband and a father at the start of Ch. 42, p. 183 and Ch. 50, p. 236?

Language techniques

Sentence structure

Well-constructed, orderly and balanced syntax is much in evidence in Austen's authorial voice and in the dialogue of the educated and intelligent characters, whose vocabulary and grammar bears a close relation to considered written language. Look, for example, at Elizabeth's advice to Jane about the Bingley family (Ch. 21, p. 96).

'...if, upon mature deliberation, you find that the misery of disobliging his two sisters is more than equivalent to the happiness of being his wife, I advise you by all means to refuse him.'

Build critical skills

Austen was influenced by her reading of essays, such as those by Swift (also a famous satirist), Addison, Johnson and Boswell. Her use of satire, and elements of style and language associated with rhetoric and debate, derive from these sources. As you read this section, make your own glossary of typical language features she employs.

Triples are frequently used for emphasis, but are also pleasing to the ear:

- Mrs Bennet 'was a woman of mean understanding, little information and uncertain temper' (Ch. 1, p. 7).
- Wickham on Georgiana Darcy: 'As a child, she was affectionate and pleasing, and extremely fond of me' (Ch. 16, p. 66). Wickham's ability to talk like an educated and moral man is an aspect of his deception.

A contrast to those who speak (and write) in this measured and sophisticated way is the flawed syntax of the foolish characters. Mrs Bennet and Lydia are obvious examples. When Lydia describes her idea of fun — as inappropriate as her flawed use of language — she says (Ch. 39. p.171):

> 'Dear me! we had such a good piece of fun the other day at Colonel Forster's…what do you think we did? We dressed up Chamberlayne in woman's clothes on purpose to pass for a lady — only think what fun! Not a soul knew of it, but Colonel and Mrs. Forster, and Kitty and me, except my aunt,…'

And Mrs Bennet reacts to Elizabeth's engagement as follows (Ch. 59, p. 292):

> 'Lord bless me! …Mr Darcy! Who would have thought it? …What pin-money, what jewels, what carriages you will have! …I am so pleased — so happy! Such a charming man!'

Punctuation — use of dashes and exclamation marks — underlines some of the characters' lack of coherent thought. **Incomplete sentences** and **vulgar expressions** are evident in both of the above quotations, where exaggeration indicates their lack of personal restraint.

The greatest contrast in use of vocabulary is between those who speak of serious moral ideas using abstract nouns (which in Austen's time would have been written with capital letters, such as Duty, Honour, Vice, Pride, further emphasising their weight), and those who reflect their limited understanding of ideas by speaking of things (for instance furniture). For example, when Darcy reflects on his upbringing (Ch. 58, p. 284) he says:

> '*Your* retrospections must be so totally void of reproach, that the contentment arising from them is not of philosophy, but, what is much better, of ignorance…Painful recollections will intrude,…I have been a selfish being all my life, in practice, though not in principle.'

Contrast this with Austen's summary of Mr Collins' description when he introduces Elizabeth to his 'humble abode' in Hunsford (Ch. 28, p. 123):

> After sitting long enough to admire every article of furniture in the room, from the sideboard to the fender…Mr. Collins invited them to take a stroll in the garden…He could number the fields in every direction, and could tell how many trees there were in the most distant clump.

Build critical skills

Compare the abstract nouns in Darcy's speech with the concrete nouns in the description of Collins. What does this imply about the intellect of each?

Any novel written more than 200 years ago must present some challenges to the reader because meanings of words change over time. When Austen uses some key words such as 'gentleman', 'civil', 'liberal', 'vulgar', or describes people passing the evening playing 'lottery' or 'loo', these words are not used in the same sense as we now understand them. Watch out for these words and other examples and find out how meanings for each differ from now.

litotes: an ironic or comic understatement in which a statement is expressed by negation of its opposite, e.g. that isn't bad — meaning it is good

Mr Collins' fake humility is also presented through his use of **litotes**, which adds to the effect of his lengthy pompous sentences. Examples are 'my proposals will not fail of being acceptable' (Ch. 19, p. 88) and 'your Hunsford visit cannot have been entirely irksome' (Ch. 38, p. 167).

Irony

Austen uses **irony** extensively. A statement is **ironic** if the truth of it is the opposite of the surface appearance.

- The unreliability of general opinion is a good example of this. If Austen puts forward the viewpoint of 'everyone' or 'all the town' has an opinion or judgement, then it will very likely be wrong, as in her opening sentence.
- In Ch. 3, judgements about Darcy change from his being 'handsomer than Mr Bingley' to 'having a most forbidding, disagreeable countenance' within a single paragraph (p. 10). Irony here lies in the capricious nature of popular opinion. What event causes the change in this case?
- On the other hand, in Ch. 18, one of the officers tells Elizabeth that Wickham is 'universally liked' (p. 73). She has had her warning.

GRADE *BOOSTER*

We see here how the narrator may inject irony into the narrative. A rather different technique is the conscious creation of a character who adds humour to the novel by speaking ironically, putting forward opinions they do not really hold. Mr Bennet does this regularly. As a reader, you need to be alert to this. In your exam, you can gain marks by explaining examples well.

Dialogue

The **conversational novel** was a recent development in the novel form which Austen adopted with enthusiasm. In all Austen's novels, a great deal of the narrative is developed through conversation and the style of the dialogue (also called **voice**) is a central method of revealing characters to the reader.

Build critical skills

Austen's novels were influenced by eighteenth-century playwrights such as Sheridan and Goldsmith. Their plays were of a genre known as 'comedy of manners', and commented satirically on the behaviour of exaggerated characters. You can see how Austen's presentation of characters engaging in conversation in social settings derives from this genre of drama. Undertake some research and list 4–5 key features of comedies of manners.

Early in the novel, we learn a great deal about all the characters in Bingley's group at Netherfield through dialogue. In Ch. 11 pp. 45–48, for example, much of what is written is dialogue. As we read, we form our opinions of the guests at Bingley's house party.

- The conversation begins with irony: Caroline Bingley puts down the book she has been pretending to read and, with a yawn, says, 'How much sooner one tires of anything but a book!' She clearly has little interest in hers. However, she goes on to comment 'When I have a house of my own, I shall be miserable if I have not an excellent library'. Earlier conversation was about Elizabeth's fondness for reading and Darcy's extensive library at Pemberley. The book Caroline has been pretending to read is the second volume of the one Darcy has chosen, so two things become clear: the first that she is trying to impress Darcy by imitation and flattery, the second that she is competing for his attention with Elizabeth. She is jealous.

- Conversation moves on to the possibility of a ball at Netherfield. Bingley's comments show him to be practical: he mentions food and invitations (concrete nouns), and says that Darcy can spend the evening in bed if he does not wish to join in.

- Caroline's next gambit to gain Darcy's attention is to ask Elizabeth to join her walking about the room. When this succeeds, he is invited to join them, but his two reasons why they would not wish him to do so show his wit and insight: either 'you have secret affairs to discuss' or 'your figures appear to the greatest advantage in walking'.

Build critical skills

Caroline's comments in Ch. 11 are a contrast with the kind of intentional irony of Mr Bennet, which is evidence of his wit. In her case, her comments are unintentionally ironic, demonstrating her lack of intellect and inviting the reader to laugh *at* her. Find further evidence of this in Caroline's dialogue.

Build critical skills

Consider how the exchange of views between Elizabeth and Darcy contributes ironically to the theme of pride.

- By contrast with Caroline, Elizabeth shows a quality we know Darcy admires: her lively mind. She is his equal in sparring with words.

- Darcy shows insight, and respect for Elizabeth's opinion, as he explores his faults. Caroline shows she has not understood the conversation and changes the subject, Bingley has nothing to contribute and Mr Hurst has been asleep, which shows that even those who do not speak can reveal some aspect of their character in a sequence of dialogue.

Build critical skills

Austen's novels adapt well to film, radio or stage partly because the dialogue can be lifted almost straight from the page into an effective script. Each character has a distinctive style of speech, from Mr Bennet's cynicism to Lady Catherine's domineering manner. How would you describe the contrasting speech styles of Mr Collins, Mary Bennet and Lydia Bennet?

Letters

The **epistolary novel**, a narrative made up entirely of letters sent between the characters, was a popular genre in the eighteenth century. Although *Pride and Prejudice* is not an epistolary novel, letters play an important part in the story. Around 40 letters are written or received and of these over ten are included in whole or part in the words of their writer.

▲ Letters are important in the novel

Letters serve four major functions for the reader. They may:

1 contain **information** about events and sometimes directly influence plot development

2 allow an author to write from a specific **viewpoint** in the first person (as 'I'), and with a specific style, thus revealing a great deal about the character of the writer (in a similar way to dialogue) and their feelings about events

3 advance certain **themes** of the novel

4 indicate the **relationship** that exists between the sender and the receiver

Darcy's letters

Darcy is shown to be a keen letter writer when he writes to his sister (Ch. 10, pp. 38–40). From his conversation with Caroline Bingley we learn that he writes regularly, at length and with care. This shows him to advantage and makes Caroline and Charles Bingley seem rather shallow by comparison.

One of Darcy's letters is presented in its entirety: the letter of explanation he sends to Elizabeth after she rejects his proposal (Ch. 35, p. 152–58). It is lengthy — so long that it is in an 'envelope'. Letters were usually just a sheet of paper folded and addressed on the blank side then sealed with sealing wax. The envelope referred to here is a folded sheet of paper enclosing the other two sheets and that was 'likewise full'.

The letter has four main functions:

1 **To reveal the character of Darcy to the reader in his own words**. Austen rarely writes from his viewpoint, and in dialogue he is not often a major contributor. The contents show him to be responsible, honest, intelligent and concerned for the welfare of others. He is anxious to explain himself to Elizabeth and answer her criticisms of his character and behaviour. His concern for Bingley's happiness is clear as is his respect for his father and care for his sister. The sincere and thoughtful tone of the letter is as important as its content in underlining the kind of man he is.

2 **To demonstrate his feelings for Elizabeth.** The agitated tone of the opening reflects his disturbed emotions. He values her sufficiently to excuse his arrogant proposal. Later in the letter, he also trusts her enough to reveal potentially damaging information about the relationship of Wickham and his sister. The letter builds more intimacy between them than his proposal of marriage, marking a turning point in the main plot as it starts the process by which Elizabeth and Darcy both begin to change in response to each other, ultimately leading to their marriage.

> **Build critical skills**
>
> The style of Darcy's letter contrasts with his usual well-constructed speech. Note the short sentences, the repetition of the word 'but' and the use of dashes, which give his words a confused and almost breathless tone. As an indication of his emotion, count how many times he says 'sorry', 'pardon' or 'apology'.

3 **To convey information that influences the plot.** The true account of Wickham's loss of support from Darcy is revealed, which foreshadows Wickham's elopement with Lydia.

4 **To develop the untrustworthiness of appearance.** Wickham is not what he had appeared to be and Elizabeth realises that Darcy is not the proud man he has seemed and is worthy of admiration. The letter also reveals Darcy's family background and contributes to the theme of family life as lived by the different characters.

Mrs Gardiner's letters

Mrs Gardiner, Elizabeth's aunt, is also shown to be a regular correspondent. She and Elizabeth write about Jane while she stays in London and share misgivings about Wickham as well as plans for their trip north. Through Mrs Gardiner's letters the reader knows her to be thoughtful, sensible and concerned for her nieces' well-being.

The most important letter she sends, though, is her reply to Elizabeth's enquiry as to what Darcy was doing at Lydia's wedding (Ch. 52, pp. 246–50). In this letter much is revealed that affects the plot: Darcy knew where to find the runaways through Mrs Younge, Georgiana's untrustworthy ex-companion. Darcy spent time meeting Wickham and a significant amount of money changed hands to ensure the pair were married.

The closeness of Mrs Gardiner's relationship with Elizabeth is stressed: she trusts her to keep this information from her mother and father, she also alludes to Darcy's probable motives for helping in such a way, ending with a request to be invited to Pemberley. The letter is another point on Elizabeth's journey towards marriage to Darcy.

Mr Collins' letters

Mr Collins' letters to Mr Bennet could not be more of a contrast with the serious correspondence above. Two of them are included in their entirety, the first as he introduces himself and announces he is to visit (Ch. 13, pp. 51–52), the second after Lydia's elopement (Ch. 48, p. 227). Both show Collins to be a pompous, priggish man, lacking the logic and self-knowledge to see the contradictions in his own writing. They help to create a caricature of the man and are a source of some sarcastic humour both to the reader and Mr Bennet.

Lydia's letters

Lydia's letters also contain elements of caricature reflecting her failures and follies. When she goes to Brighton, she writes infrequently and briefly to her parents, though it later turns out she has been writing in more detail to Kitty, letters said to be 'too full of lines under the words

Build critical skills

Just as dialogue can be a source of humour, so are letters written by comic characters. Here too exaggeration and satire are in evidence. Find three examples of Austen's use of this technique.

to be made public'. Lydia's extravagant style of writing and outrageous comments reflect the silly, unguarded nature of her conversation.

Two complete letters are included: her farewell note to Mrs Forster when she left Brighton with Wickham (Ch. 47, p. 223) and her congratulations to Elizabeth (Ch. 61, p. 298).

Description

By comparison with many writers, there is little in the way of physical description of people or places in Austen's novels, but note how Austen uses precise vocabulary and syntax to conjure up people and settings.

Descriptions of people

We are largely left to imagine for ourselves what characters look like. Remarks from other characters or the authorial voice provide incidental details, such as Darcy's height and seriousness, Elizabeth's 'fine eyes' and tanned complexion, Jane's reputation as a beauty, Lydia's being 'tall and well-grown'.

Austen uses little imagery in the sense of similes and metaphors, but she does build up 'word pictures' to help readers understand a personality. Her distinctive style allows her to sum up a character in a few well-chosen words.

● She chooses **precise adjectives** to describe characters' actions and thoughts. Note how she uses **lists and triples**.

● She emphasises details about a character by saying **what they are not**, or by contrast with someone else.

Descriptions of settings

Places are important in *Pride and Prejudice* as the action moves from fictional towns and villages (like Meryton and Longbourn) in the real county of Hertfordshire, to real streets in London, to Kent and back into fiction (at Hunsford parsonage and the estate at Rosings). Sometimes names of towns are given simply as blanks, indicating a real town but one the author has chosen not to identify, though at other times larger towns such as Newcastle and Brighton are named. When the Gardiners journey to Derbyshire, Austen lists real towns they pass through (Oxford, Blenheim, Warwick, Kenilworth, Birmingham (Ch. 42, p. 186) but invents the village of Lampton and Darcy's estate at Pemberley.

It seems that Austen worked with a map to locate her geographical settings much as she worked with a calendar to plot the sequence of events. Even so, like her characters, the places are rarely described in any detail, with a few exceptions, for example, the parsonage at Hunsford and the grand house at Rosings, which are revealed through Mr Collins' admiring descriptions.

Key quotation

'I am going to Gretna Green…I shall send for my clothes when I get to Longbourn; but I wish you would tell Sally to mend a great slit in my worked muslin gown before they are packed up.'

Lydia's priorities as she prepares to elope (Ch.47, p. 223)

Key quotation

Mr. Collins, to be sure, was neither sensible nor agreeable; his society was irksome, and his attachment to her must be imaginary. But still, he would be her husband.

Charlotte's thoughts about her intended husband (Ch. 22, p. 98)

Build critical skills

Compare the description of Mr Collins to the authorial introduction to Lady Catherine (Ch. 29, p. 127) and to Colonel Fitzwilliam (Ch. 30, p. 134). What distinctive features of style can you identify from these descriptions?

It was a large, handsome, stone building, standing well on rising ground, and backed by a ridge of high woody hills; — and in front, a stream of some natural importance was swelled into greater, but without any artificial appearance. Its banks were neither formal, nor falsely adorned.

(Ch. 43, p. 187)

Pemberley

The most detailed description of any place is to be found when Elizabeth visits Pemberley, which represents a crucial turning point in the development of her feelings for Darcy. The fact that Austen gives so much detail is significant, for the description symbolises Darcy himself. This description, and the use of the seasons as a background for events (see 'Plot and structure', p. 27), are the most obvious evidence of symbolism in this novel.

Build critical skills

Consider less significant details which could have a symbolic purpose. What do you make of the palings (fencing) surrounding the park at Rosings or Elizabeth's soiled petticoat? Add any other references to clothing or to places which could be interpreted as symbolic.

GRADE FOCUS

Grade 5

Students will be able to identify a range of aspects of language and structure, for example, explaining how rhetorical devices communicate something about a character or a theme. They will comment clearly on how dialogue develops plot and character, with relevant evidence selected from the text. Literary terminology will be used with clarity.

Grade 8

Students will offer a perceptive and sustained appreciation of a variety of features of language and structure. They will need to show an increasingly sophisticated evaluation and analysis of evidence to reach the highest grades. Literary critical terminology will be used with precision.

REVIEW YOUR LEARNING

(Answers are given on pages 111–112.)

1   What is an epistolary novel, and how is *Pride and Prejudice* influenced by this genre?
2   How is dialogue used to present characters to the reader?
3   Name three techniques used to incorporate humour into the novel.
4   Name three rhetorical devices Austen uses.
5   How does Jane Austen change the viewpoint used to communicate the narrative? Explain three techniques she uses to do this.
6   Where is symbolism used in *Pride and Prejudice*?
7   What stylistic technique does Jane Austen use instead of imagery?

Tackling the exams

Target your thinking

- What sorts of questions will you have to answer?
- What is the best way to plan and structure your answer?
- How can you improve your grade?
- What do you have to do to achieve the highest grade?

Your response to a question on *Pride and Prejudice* will be assessed in a 'closed book' English Literature examination, which means that you are not allowed to take copies of the text into the examination room. Different examination boards will test you in different ways and it is vital that you know on which paper the nineteenth-century novel will be and the sort of question you will be answering, so that you can be well prepared on the day of the examination.

Whichever exam board you are following, the table on the next page explains which paper and section the novel appears in and gives you information about the sort of question you will face and how you will be assessed.

Marking

The marking of your responses varies according to the board your school or you have chosen. Each exam board will have a slightly different mark scheme, consisting of a ladder of grades. The marks you achieve in each part of the examination will be converted to your final overall grade. Grades are numbered from 1–9, with 9 being the highest.

It is important that you familiarise yourself with the relevant mark scheme(s) for your examination. Assessment Objectives (AOs) or individual assessments are explained in the next section of the guide.

Approaching the examination question

First impressions

First read the whole question and make sure you understand exactly what the task requires you to do. It is very easy in the highly pressured atmosphere of the examination room to misread a question and this can be disastrous. Under no circumstances should you try and twist the question to the one that you have spent hours revising or the one you answered brilliantly in your mock exam.

> **GRADE BOOSTER**
>
> Make sure you read carefully any additional advice, explanation or bullet points. They are there to help and guide you.

	AQA	Edexcel	OCR	Eduqas
Paper and section	Paper 1 Section B	Paper 2 Section A	Paper 1 Section B	Paper 2 Section B
Type of question	Extract-based question requiring a response to an aspect of the extract and a response to the same or similar aspect in the novel as a whole.	Two-part question. Part a) is based on an extract, requiring a close response to language. Part b) requires a response to an aspect elsewhere in the novel.	Either an extract-based question requiring a response to an aspect of the extract and the same aspect elsewhere in the novel, or an essay question requiring a response to 'moments' chosen from the novel.	Extract-based question requiring response to an aspect of the extract and the same or similar aspect in the novel as a whole.
Closed book?	Yes	Yes	Yes	Yes
Choice of question?	No	No	Yes	No
Paper and section length	Paper 1 = 1 hour 45 minutes Section B = approx. 50 minutes	Paper 2 = 2 hours 15 minutes Section A = 55 minutes	Paper 1 = 2 hours Section B = 45 minutes	Paper 2 = 2 hours 30 minutes Section B = approx. 45 minutes
% of whole grade	20%	25%	25%	20%
AOs assessed	AO1 AO2 AO3	Part a): AO2 Part b): AO1	AO1 AO2 AO3 AO4	AO1 AO2 AO3
Is AO4 (SPaG) assessed in this section?	No	No	Yes	No

SPaG: spelling, punctuation and grammar

Are you being asked to think about how a character or theme is being presented or is the question about setting or atmosphere? Make sure you know so that you will be able to sustain your focus later.

As you can see from the table opposite, all four exam boards offer *Pride and Prejudice* as a text, and all offer an extract-based question. However, the wordings and formats of the questions are slightly different. The extract will be linked to one or two tasks that you are required to complete.

As a starting point, you may wish to underline keywords in the question, such as 'how' to remind you to write about methods and any other words which you feel will help you to focus on answering the question you are being asked. Below are examples of the question types from each examination board which have been annotated in this way.

AQA

Starting with this extract, write about <u>how</u> Austen presents <u>attitudes towards marriage</u> in the novel.

Write about:

- <u>how</u> Austen presents <u>attitudes towards marriage in the extract</u>
- <u>how</u> Austen presents <u>attitudes towards marriage in the novel as a whole</u>

[30 marks]

Eduqas

You should use the extract and your knowledge of the whole novel to answer this question.

Write about <u>attitudes towards marriage</u> in *Pride and Prejudice* and <u>how</u> they are shown in the novel.

In your response you should:

- refer to the <u>extract</u> and the <u>novel as a whole</u>;
- show your understanding of <u>attitudes towards marriage</u> in the novel;
- refer to the <u>contexts</u> of the novel.

[40 marks]

Edexcel

In Ch. 22 Charlotte Lucas and Elizabeth Bennet discuss Charlotte's engagement to Mr Collins.

(a) Explore <u>how</u> Austen presents Charlotte and Elizabeth's <u>attitudes towards marriage</u> in this extract.

Give <u>examples from the extract</u> to support your ideas.

(20)

(b) In this extract, contrasting attitudes to marriage are presented. Explain how the theme of marriage is explored **elsewhere** in the novel.

In your answer you must consider:

● the importance of marriage in the novel

● the contrasting attitudes to marriage that are shown.

(20)

(Total for Question 5 = 40 marks)

OCR

EITHER

Explore how Austen presents contrasts in Charlotte Lucas' and Elizabeth Bennet's attitudes towards marriage in this extract and elsewhere in the novel.

[40]

OR

How does Jane Austen make Mr Collins a humorous character in the novel? Explore at least two moments from the novel to support your ideas.

[40]

(NB: for OCR, the alternative essay question will not be related to the extract.)

Spot the differences

● AQA and Eduqas do not divide the answer into sections. Both ask for reference to the '**whole novel**'.

● OCR also does not divide the answer into sections. The question will ask you to select evidence from the extract and '**elsewhere in the novel**'.

● Only Edexcel has a two-part question. In part a) of the question, marks are awarded for AO2 only. Part b) will require you to write about an aspect linked to the extract, using the phrase '**elsewhere in the novel**', and awards marks only to AO1.

● Only Eduqas refers directly to 'contexts' in the question, and awards a third of the marks to AO3.

● Only Edexcel does not assess AO3 in this section.

● Only OCR gives you a choice of an extract-based question *or* an essay unrelated to the extract.

● Only OCR awards marks to AO4 in this question.

GRADE BOOSTER

All four boards assess both AO1 and AO2 in this section of the paper. Always make sure you cover both of these AOs in your response, even if they do not seem to be signposted clearly in the question.

'Working' the text

- If you answering a question where you are provided with an extract, your first step is to *read the passage* very carefully, trying to get an overview or general impression of what is going on, and what or who is being described.

- Then *read* the passage again, underlining or highlighting any words or short phrases that you think might be related to the focus of the question and are of special interest. For example, they might be surprising, unusual or amusing. You might have a strong emotional or analytical reaction to them, or you might think that they are particularly clever or noteworthy.

- To gain high marks for an AO2 response, you have to consider how words and phrases may work together to produce a particular effect or to get you to think about a particular theme, and you have to explore the methods the writer uses to present a character in a particular way for their own purposes.

- You may pick out examples of literary techniques such as lists or use of irony, or sound effects such as alliteration. You may spot an unusual word order, sentence construction or use of punctuation.

Planning your answer

It is advisable to write a brief plan before you start writing your response to avoid repeating yourself or getting into a muddle. A plan is not a first draft: you will not have time to draft. In fact, if your plan consists of full sentences at all, you are probably eating into the time you have available for writing a really insightful and considered answer. However, a plan is important because it helps you to gather and organise your thoughts, but it should consist of brief words and phrases.

You may find it helpful to use a diagram of some sort — perhaps a **spider diagram** or **flow chart**. This may help you to keep your mind open to new ideas as you plan, so that you can slot them in. You could make a list instead. The important thing is to choose a method that works for you.

If you have made a spider diagram, arranging your thoughts is a simple matter of numbering the branches in the best possible order.

Writing your answer

Now you are ready to start writing your answer. Remember that you are working against the clock and so it is really important to use your time wisely.

You may not have time to deal with all of the points you wish to make in your response. If you simply identify several language features and make a brief comment on each, you will be working at a fairly low level.

> **GRADE BOOSTER**
>
> When you start writing you must try to explain the effects created by particular words/phrases or techniques, and not simply identify what they mean. AO2, the Assessment Objective concerned with language, is worth a high proportion of the marks, so your answer will have to demonstrate your understanding of how Austen's use of dialogue, choice of viewpoint, irony, caricature and so on help to communicate her message to the reader.

The idea is to **select** the ones that you find most interesting and develop them in a sustained and detailed manner. In order to move up the levels in the mark scheme, it is important to write a lot about a little, rather than a little about a lot.

You must also remember to address the whole question as you will be penalised if you fail to do so.

If you have any time left at the end of the examination, do not waste it. Check carefully that your meaning is clear and that you have done the very best that you can. Look back at your plan and check that you have included all your best points. Is there anything else you can add? Keep thinking until you are told to put your pen down!

Referring to the author and title

You can refer to Austen either by name (make sure you spell it correctly) or as 'the writer'. You should never use her first name (Jane) — this sounds as if you know her personally. You can save time by giving the novel title in full the first time you refer to it, and afterwards simply referring to it as 'the novel'.

GRADE *BOOSTER*

Do not lose sight of the author in your essay. Remember that the novel is a construct — the characters, their thoughts, their words, their actions have all been created by Austen — so most of your points should be about what Austen might have been trying to achieve. In explaining how her message is conveyed to you, for instance through description of an event, through dialogue involving a character, use of symbolism, irony and so on, don't forget to mention her name. For example:

- Austen makes it clear that...
- It is evident from...that Austen is inviting the reader to consider...
- Here, the reader may well feel that Austen is suggesting...

Writing in an appropriate style

Remember that you are expected to write in a suitable register. This means that you need to use an appropriate style. This means:

- *Not* using colloquial language or slang, e.g. 'Mr Darcy is a right snob, so up himself he deserves everyone to diss him.'

- *Not* becoming too personal or anecdotal, e.g. 'Charles reminds me of my Uncle Craig, life and soul of the party, like when my cousin Kelly got married he danced all night with everyone.'

- Using suitable phrases for an academic essay, e.g. 'It could be argued that', not 'I reckon that...' or 'Lady Catherine's words give the reader the impression that...' rather than 'This quote shows that...'.

- *Not* being too dogmatic. Don't say 'This means that...'. It is much better to say, 'This might suggest that...'.

You are also expected to be able to use a range of technical terms correctly. The 'Language, style and analysis' section of this guide should help with that. However, if you cannot remember the correct name for a technique but can still explain the effect it creates, you should go ahead and do so.

The first person ('I')

It is perfectly appropriate to say 'I feel' or 'I think'. You are being asked for your opinion. Just remember that you are being asked for your opinion about *what* Austen may have been trying to convey in her novel (her themes and ideas) and *how* she does this (through characters, events, language, form and structure of the novel).

Spelling, punctuation and grammar (AO4)

Although your spelling, punctuation and grammar are **not** specifically targeted for assessment on the nineteenth-century novel (unless you are taking the OCR exam, where each question has a small number of marks allocated to accuracy), you cannot afford to forget that you will demonstrate your grasp of the novel through the accuracy of what you write, so take great care with this and don't be sloppy. If the examiner cannot understand what you are trying to say, they will not be able to give you credit for it.

How to raise your grade

- Answer the question in front of you. You need to start doing this straight away. You have only a short time in this exam, so get started as soon as you have gathered your thoughts together and made a brief plan.

- Sometimes students go into panic mode because they don't know how to start. It is absolutely fine to begin an extract-based response with the words, 'In this extract Austen presents...'.

- Pick out interesting words and phrases and unpick or explore them within the context or focus of the question. For example, if the question is about the way the theme of marriage is presented, you need to focus on picking out words and phrases to do with contrasting ideas about marriage.

GRADE BOOSTER

If you can't remember the exact name for a device such as 'litotes' or 'antithesis', you could just refer to it as a rhetorical device.

GRADE BOOSTER

Make the quotations you select brief and try to embed them. This will save you time and help you develop your points at greater depth, e.g. 'Jane's letters at first judge Wickham to be "thoughtless and indiscreet... nothing bad at heart". However, even Jane agrees he is "not a man to be trusted" once she learns the whole story.'

- What methods has the writer used? It might be something as simple as a powerful adjective. What do you think is the impact of that word? It might be that the word you are referring to has more than one meaning. If that is the case, the examiner will be impressed if you can discuss what the word means to you, but can also suggest other meanings.

- Is context relevant? In other words, would Austen's readers view marriage differently? What might Austen have been trying to express about a particular attitude to marriage when she chose this word or phrase?

- It is likely that you will find it easier to address AO2 (methods) when writing about the extract as you have the actual words to hand. Is there an overall effect? For instance, you may have noticed Austen's frequent use of lists (or triples) of adjectives or noun phrases which help create your impressions of a character. As well as analysing individual words in the list you could also describe the cumulative effect.

- Be very careful about lapsing into narrative, or writing about a character as if he or she is a real person. If you are asked about how Austen presents a comic character like Mr Collins, remember that the focus of the question is about the methods that Austen uses. Do not simply tell the examiner what Collins does or what he is like — this is a very common mistake.

Remember all the exam boards ask you to deal with the focus of the question in 'the novel as a whole' or 'elsewhere in the novel'. If you feel you have more to offer in terms of comments on the extract, leave a space so that you can return to it if you have time after dealing with other parts of the novel.

Key points to remember

- Do not just jump straight in. Spending time wisely in those first moments may gain you extra marks later.

- Write a brief plan.

- Remember to answer the question.

- Refer closely to *details* in the passage in your answer, support your comments, and remember you must also refer to 'the novel as a whole' or refer to 'elsewhere' in the novel.

- Use your time wisely. Try to leave a few minutes to look back over your work and check your spelling, punctuation and grammar, so that your meaning is clear and so that you know you have done the very best that you can.

- Keep an eye on the clock.

GRADE FOCUS

Grade 5

Students will have a clear focus on the text and the task and will be able to 'read between the lines'. They will develop a clear understanding of the ways in which writers use language, form and structure to create effects for the readers. They will use a range of detailed textual evidence to support comments. They will show understanding of the idea that both writers and readers may be influenced by where, when and why a text is produced.

Grade 8

Students will produce a consistently convincing, informed response to a range of meanings and ideas within the text. They will use ideas which are well-linked and will often build on one another. They will dig deep into the text, examining, exploring and evaluating the writer's use of language, form and structure. They will carefully select finely judged textual references which are well integrated in order to support and develop their response to the text. They will show perceptive understanding of how contexts shape texts and responses to texts.

Aiming for a Grade 9

To reach the very highest level you need to have thought about the novel more deeply and produce a response which is conceptualised, critical and exploratory at a deeper level. You might, for instance, challenge accepted critical views in evaluating the impact of her writing. If, for example, you think Austen was more influenced by Romanticism than most critics imply, where do you find evidence of this and what message do you think she is conveying to the reader?

You may feel, for example, that both Elizabeth and Darcy present challenges to conventional nineteenth century thinking about gender roles, social class and marriage, points which have limited impact on a modern reader. Do you consider this a problem or not?

REVIEW YOUR LEARNING

(Answers are given on p. 112.)

1 On which paper is your *Pride and Prejudice* question?

2 Can you take your copy of the novel into the exam?

3 Will you have a choice of question?

4 How long do you have to answer the question?

5 What advice would you give to another student about using quotations?

6 Will you be assessed on spelling, punctuation and grammar in your response to *Pride and Prejudice*?

7 Why is it important to plan your answer?

8 What should you do if you finish ahead of time?

Assessment Objectives and skills

All GCSE examinations are pinned to specific areas of learning that the examiners want to be sure the candidates have mastered. These are known as Assessment Objectives or AOs. The examiner marking your response will be using the particular mark scheme for that board, but all mark schemes are based on fulfilling the key AOs for English Literature.

Let's break the Assessment Objectives down to see what they really mean.

> **AO1** Read, understand and respond to texts. Students should be able to:
> - maintain a critical style and develop an informed personal response
> - use textual references, including quotations, to support and illustrate interpretations.

At its most basic level, this AO is about having a good grasp of what a text is about and being able to express an opinion about it within the context of the question. For example, if you were to say, 'The novel is about the development of an unlikely romance between a very rich gentlemen, Darcy, and a spirited young woman, Elizabeth' you would be beginning to address AO1 because you have made a personal response. An 'informed' response refers to the basis on which you make that judgement. In other words, you need to show that you know the novel well enough to answer the question.

It is closely linked to the idea that you are also required to '**use textual references including quotations to support and illustrate interpretations**'. This means giving short direct quotations from the text. For example, if you wanted to support the idea that Elizabeth is spirited, you could use a direct quote to point to her response to Darcy's insult (at the ball in Meryton) demonstrating her 'lively playful disposition, which delighted in anything ridiculous'. Alternatively, you can simply refer to details in the text, in order to support your views. So you might say: 'Elizabeth's response to Darcy's slight is to amuse her friends with a witty retelling of the event.'

Note that AO1 asks for exam candidates to write in a 'critical style'. Technical accuracy is not allocated any marks on this question (except a small percentage for OCR) but adopting an appropriately formal register and writing fluently will gain AO1 marks.

Generally speaking, most candidates find AO1 relatively easy. Usually, it is tackled well — if you answer the question you are asked and write well, this AO will probably take care of itself.

> **AO2** Analyse the language, form and structure used by a writer to create meanings and effects, using relevant subject terminology where appropriate.

AO2 is not as easy as AO1. Most examiners would probably agree that covering AO2 is a weakness for many candidates, particularly those students who only ever talk about the characters as if they were real people.

In simple terms, AO2 refers to the writer's methods and is often signposted in questions by the word 'how' or the phrase 'how does the writer present...?'.

Overall, AO2 is easily overlooked, so it is vital that you are fully aware of this objective. The word '**language**' refers to Austen's use of words, authorial methods or style. Remember that writers choose words very carefully in order to achieve particular effects. They may spend quite a long time deciding between two or three words which are similar in meaning in order to create the precise effect that they are looking for.

If you are addressing AO2 in your response to *Pride and Prejudice*, you will typically find yourself using Austen's name and exploring the choices she has made. For example, Austen describes Elizabeth's enjoyment of 'anything ridiculous' and quoting this will set you on the right path to explaining why these word are an interesting choice to present the reader with her reaction to Darcy's ill-mannered comment. It is this explanation that addresses AO2, whilst 'Elizabeth "had a lively playful disposition"' is a simple AO1 comment.

Language also encompasses a wide range of writer's methods, such as the use of different points of view, symbolism, irony, caricature.

AO2 also refers to your use of '**subject terminology**'. This means that you should be able to use terms such as 'unreliable narrator', 'litotes' and 'hyperbole' with confidence and understanding. However, if you can't remember the term, don't despair — you will still gain marks for explaining the effects being created.

The terms '**form**' and '**structure**' refer to the kind of text you are studying and how it has been 'put together' by the writer. This might include the narrative technique being used. In *Pride and Prejudice* Austen uses the third person intrusive narrator and tells a great deal of the story through dialogue between its various characters. Aspects of form include the genre(s) the text is part of; structure includes the order of events and the effects created, for example the way key events are juxtaposed. You might write about contrasts offered between romantic and family relationships as Austen develops the novel's main themes, or the pattern of repeated proposals of marriage. Effects of structure can also be seen in the writer's use of sentence lengths and word order (syntax).

Remember: if you do not address AO2 at all, it will be very difficult to achieve much higher than grade 1, since you will not be answering the question.

> **AO3** Show understanding of the relationship between texts and the contexts in which they were written.

Although AO3 is perhaps not considered as important as AO1 and AO2, is still worth between 15% and 20% of your total mark and so should not be underestimated. You need to check your exam board to see what proportion of the AO3 marks are given to the question on *Pride and Prejudice*. This could be as much as one-third of the marks on the nineteenth-century novel question if your board is Eduqas, but no marks if you are entered with Edexcel.

To cover AO3 you must show that you understand the links between a text and when, why and for whom it was written. For example, some awareness of expectations about romantic relationships and marriage in Regency England (the historical and social context) may well help you to understand Austen's intentions in writing *Pride and Prejudice* to fuel debate and perhaps even change the attitudes of her middle- and upper-class readership. Equally, some knowledge of Austen's background and the reading she undertook herself might give you useful insight into her interest in the literary movements of the eighteenth and early nineteenth century (the literary and cultural context).

However, it is important to understand that context should not be 'bolted on' to your response for no good reason; you are writing about literature not history.

> **AO4** Use a range of vocabulary and sentence structures for clarity, purpose and effect, with accurate spelling and punctuation.

This AO is fairly self-explanatory and it is worth remembering that it will be assessed on some of your exam essays, though is NOT assessed in your response to *Pride and Prejudice* unless your exam board is OCR.

However, a clear and well-written response should always be your aim. If your spelling is so poor or your grammar and lack of punctuation so confusing that the examiner cannot understand what you are trying to express, this will obviously adversely affect your mark.

Similarly, although there are no marks awarded for good handwriting, and none taken away for untidiness or crossings outs, it is obviously important for the examiner to be able to read what you have written. If you believe your handwriting is so illegible that it may cause difficulties for the examiner, you need to speak to your schools examination officer in plenty of time before the exam. He or she may be able to arrange for you to have a scribe or to sit your examination using a computer.

Common mistakes

- **Retelling the story.** You can be sure that the examiner marking your response knows the story inside out. A key feature of the lowest grades is 'retelling the story'. Don't do it.

- **Quoting long passages.** Remember that every reference and quotation must serve a very specific point you are making. If you quote at length, the examiner will have to guess which bit of the quotation you mean to serve your point. Copying out large chunks of an extract is a waste of time, and trying to quote at any length from a novel when you don't have the book to refer to is likely to lead to misquoting. Neither is going to gain you marks. Keep quotations short and smart.

- **Merely identifying literary devices.** You will never gain marks simply for identifying literary devices such as hyperbole or irony. Similarly you will gain no marks for pointing out that 'Austen uses a lot of adjectives in this sentence'. However, you can gain marks by identifying these features, exploring the reasons why you think the author has used them and offering a thoughtful consideration of how they might impact on readers, as well as an evaluation of how effective you think they are.

- **Giving unsubstantiated opinions.** The examiner will be keen to give you marks for your opinions, but only if they are supported by reasoned argument and references to the text (see AO1 above). So, no marks for writing 'Everyone thinks Lydia is completely stupid, but I don't'. You will be rewarded though for a comment which refers to detail from the novel, such as: 'It is easy to dismiss Lydia as having poor judgement and little common sense. However, Austen presents her as sharing Elizabeth's capacity for fun and enjoyment of life. Unfortunately, she is shown to lack Elizabeth's intellect and the kind of guidance from her parents that her immaturity calls for.'

- **Writing about characters as if they are real people.** It is important to remember that characters are constructs — the writer is responsible for what the characters do and say. Don't ignore the author!

REVIEW YOUR LEARNING

(Answers are given on p. 112.)

1 How many Assessment Objectives are there?

2 What does AO1 assess?

3 What sort of material do you need to cover to successfully address AO2?

4 What aspects of the text should you write about to gain AO3 marks? Is AO3 assessed in your *Pride and Prejudice* answer?

5 What aspects of your writing does AO4 cover? Is it assessed in your *Pride and Prejudice* answer?

6 Which exam board specification are you following and what AOs should you be focusing on?

7 What should you *not* do in your responses?

Sample essays

Target your thinking

- What features does a grade 5 essay have?
- How does a grade 8 essay improve on that?
- What makes for a good introduction and conclusion?
- What is an 'appropriate' essay style?

AQA sample question and response

The question below is typical of an AQA character-based question which requires you to consider both an extract and the novel as a whole.

> Read the following extract from Chapter 15 then answer the question that follows.
>
> In this extract Elizabeth and her sisters meet Mr Wickham for the first time, as they walk in the town of Meryton.

But the attention of every lady was soon caught by a young man, whom they had never seen before, of most gentlemanlike appearance, walking with another officer on the other side of the way. The officer was the very Mr. Denny concerning whose return from London Lydia came to inquire, and he bowed as they passed. All were struck with the stranger's air, all wondered who he could be, and Kitty and Lydia, determined if possible to find out, led the way across the street, under pretence of wanting something in an opposite shop, and fortunately had just gained the pavement when the two gentlemen turning back had reached the same spot. Mr. Denny addressed them directly, and entreated permission to introduce his friend, Mr. Wickham, who had returned with him the day before from town, and he was happy to say had accepted a commission in their corps. This was exactly as it should be; for the young man wanted only regimentals to make him completely charming. His appearance was greatly in his favour; he had all the best part of beauty, a fine countenance, a good figure, and very pleasing address. The introduction was followed up on his side by a happy readiness of conversation—a readiness at the same time perfectly correct and unassuming; and the whole party were still standing and talking together very agreeably, when the sound of horses drew their notice, and Darcy and Bingley were seen riding down the street. On distinguishing the ladies of the group, the two gentlemen came directly towards them, and began the usual civilities. Bingley was the principal spokesman, and Miss Bennet the principal object. He was then, he said, on his way to Longbourn on purpose to inquire after her. Mr. Darcy corroborated it with a bow, and was beginning to determine not to fix his eyes on Elizabeth, when they were suddenly arrested by the sight of the stranger, and Elizabeth happening to see the countenance of both as they looked at each other, was all astonishment at the effect of the meeting. Both changed colour, one looked white, the other red. Mr. Wickham, after a few moments, touched his hat—a salutation which Mr. Darcy just deigned to return. What could be the meaning of it? It was impossible to imagine; it was impossible not to long to know.

Starting with this extract, write about how Austen presents Elizabeth's impressions of Mr George Wickham.

Write about:

- how Austen presents Elizabeth's first impressions of Mr Wickham in this extract
- how Austen presents changing impressions of Mr Wickham in the novel as a whole

[30 marks — AO1 and AO2 12 marks each, AO3 6 marks]

Below are exam responses from two students working at different levels. They cover much the same points. However, you should be able to see how Student Y takes similar material to that of Student X, but develops it further in order to achieve a higher grade.

In addressing the first bullet, both students looked at the extract and began by considering how Elizabeth's first impressions of Wickham's character and appearance are presented.

Student X, who is likely to achieve grade 5, begins the response like this:

> In this extract Austen introduces George Wickham into the novel as a rival to Darcy, but as the story goes on we learn that he is not what he first seems to be. This whole paragraph is third person authorial narrative from different points of view, some from Elizabeth. Although conversation is summarised there is no actual dialogue in the extract, which is quite unusual in this novel. To begin with all four sisters, including Elizabeth are taken in by his good looks, 'a fine countenance, a good figure, and very pleasing address.' There is no clue at all to what he is really like.

1 Clear focus on task — extract and whole text (AO1).

2 Identification of authorial methods (AO2) but no real analysis as yet.

3 Effective textual reference (AO1), but level 5 because it fails to read between the lines regarding the mysterious exchange of looks between Wickham and Darcy (AO2).

Student Y, who is likely to achieve grade 8, begins the response like this:

> George Wickham is introduced in this chapter as Darcy's rival for Elizabeth's affection, though right from the outset Austen hints that he is not what he seems to be. Jane Austen's narrative method is engaging for the reader as she keeps us guessing whether to agree with Elizabeth that he is just the man for her, or whether her 'first impression' of him is as misguided as of Darcy. Austen's original title for this novel, interestingly, was 'First Impressions.'

1 Strong introduction — no time wasted in establishing the topic — and comment about extract and whole text already evident.

2 Understanding of authorial method (AO2), but no specific analysis yet. Hints at understanding of a central theme which is developed in the essay (AO1 and AO2).

3 An important and relevant observation links the novel's original title with the wording of this task.

Both students continue by looking in detail at how Austen presents Wickham's appearance and character in the extract.

Student X writes:

1 Relevant quoted evidence (AO1). Contextual aspect could be mentioned (AO3).

2 Understanding of language detail/authorial methods (AO2).

3 Clear point of contrast made between the two men with relevant textual reference (AO1).

4 Inference — clear interpretation of textual detail (AO1).

5 Good point, but too informal (AO1) and ambiguous as to which of the two goes white (AO1).

When he first appears he is planning to join the army: 'the young man wanted only regimentals to make him completely charming'. This shows, in the girls' opinion, he will be completely perfect once he is in an army uniform. To begin with the narrative point of view is of 'every lady', so this probably means Lydia and Kitty more than Elizabeth. He is described as being 'gentlemanlike' which maybe is Austen hinting that he is not a real gentleman, like Darcy is. His behaviour is the opposite of Darcy. Wickham has 'happy readiness of conversation...perfectly correct and unassuming' and this is what appeals to Elizabeth. At the end of this extract Darcy is awkward and doesn't speak at all, though it hints that he is secretly interested in Elizabeth as he 'was beginning to determine not to fix his eyes on Elizabeth'. From her point of view this just looks like rudeness.

There is one weird moment when Darcy notices who Wickham is and 'one looked white, the other red' but you can't work out why.

Student Y writes:

The extract is a paragraph written entirely in the third person, firstly from a fairly general viewpoint of 'every lady'. This could be a sign from Austen that the judgements made are misguided, as elsewhere in the novel, general opinion tends to be erroneous. Wickham is also described here with elements of irony: having a 'most gentlemanlike appearance' and '…[wanting] only regimentals to make him completely charming', which also alerts the reader into questioning whether his appearance may be deceptive. A soldier's uniform might well make him look very handsome to a certain shallow type of girl (for example Lydia), but the man beneath matters more than his 'charming' appearance.

Authorial comment proclaims him to have 'a happy readiness of conversation…perfectly correct and unassuming', though no actual dialogue is used, which is also unusual in this novel where we are usually invited to form our impressions of characters from their own words. The end of the extract takes the reader to Elizabeth's viewpoint, as she will see the direct contrast with the taciturn Mr Darcy, presumably making a positive impression on her, though her curiosity is aroused as Wickham goes oddly silent when Darcy appears and 'Both changed colour, one looked white, the other red'. Both Elizabeth and the reader want to find out what has happened between the two: Austen's question and the intriguing antithetical sentence which concludes the extract ensure that we will read on with anticipation.

1 Insightful awareness and evaluation of authorial methods (AO2).

2 Selection of precise evidence and critical commentary (AO1 and AO2).

3 Authorial methods explored (AO2).

4 Skilfully integrated quotation — sustained focus on the question (AO1) and good analysis of stylistic significance of evidence (AO2).

The students then move on to respond to the second part of the question — how Elizabeth's attitude to Wickham is further developed in 'the novel as a whole'.

Student X continues:

1 Relevant evidence selected, but incomplete understanding — in 1800, 'gallantry' implied an eye for the ladies (AO2 and AO3).

2 Clear reference to authorial device and language effects with well-chosen textual evidence (AO1 and AO2).

Austen shows us just how Wickham sets his sights on Elizabeth and he talks to her a lot and Elizabeth trusts him. It says he talks with 'gallantry' which implies he is a very pleasant man and the opposite of Darcy. Austen uses dialogue to show what a persuasive talker he is and how he shows himself in a good light by using positive emotive words and intensifiers, like 'excessively attached' and 'provide for me amply.' Because she is prejudiced against Darcy, Elizabeth believes every word of the story of how Darcy stopped him getting the money he was promised. He says that the late Mr Darcy intended to give him money and a position in the church for him but that Darcy got all the money by fault.

This makes Darcy out to be the bad guy to the reader as well as Elizabeth and makes Wickham sound like the victim. Wickham says he has a 'warm unguarded temper' which also makes him sound favourable and a contrast to Darcy.

The bad things about Wickham are all told by other people and a lot of it is in letters. For example, Darcy writes a letter to explain to Elizabeth what Wickham really did and how he chose to go into the law instead of the church, then wasted £1,000 by 'a life of idleness' and gambling. It is obvious why Darcy did not let him have the position his father promised. Then he tried to run off with Darcy's sister and she was only 15. He was obviously after her money, just as he was with the heiress Miss King.

3 Clear point — relating events to a major theme of the novel (AO1).

4 Wrong word ('default' would be correct) — and the sentence that follows is inappropriate in style (AO1).

5 Understanding of the purpose of the letters (AO2).

6 A clear point, with relevant textual support, though the sum of money is inaccurate.

7 Clumsy expression reduces the impact this paragraph ending could have had (AO1).

Austen writes from Elizabeth's point of view about how she feels cheated, foolish and embarrassed, and her big mistake is that she doesn't let anyone except Jane know any of this, so no one thinks twice when Lydia keeps talking about Wickham, and then she is allowed to go to Brighton when his regiment goes there.

1 Authorial method identified (AO2), though slipping into story-telling and irrelevance — losing focus of HOW Austen shows us Elizabeth's impression of Wickham.

Next thing we know, Elizabeth gets a letter from Jane saying that Wickham and Lydia have eloped to Gretna Green to get married, but he is even worse than that, he just goes to live with Lydia in London, which would have been extremely shocking in those days, as respectable unmarried couples did not live together.

2 Social context hinted at but undeveloped (AO3).

Student X concludes like this:

Mrs Gardiner's letters tell how much it cost Darcy to persuade Wickham to marry Lydia: £1,000 each year 'settled on Lydia' and then to pay off gambling debts 'considerably more than a thousand pounds.' All the facts about money Austen uses to show just how much of a fortune hunter Wickham is.

1 A clear point with relevant textual support, though the sum of money is inaccurate. Clumsy expression lessens the impact of the paragraph (AO1).

The last time he is mentioned is at the very end when Austen narrates how he is always in debt, so he and Lydia depend on Elizabeth and Darcy for money and Bingley and Jane for somewhere to live. The change in Elizabeth's impression of him makes the reader understand how he is really bad and completely different from the 'gentleman' he seemed to be to start with.

2 Clear awareness of authorial method (AO2).

3 Clear conclusion — sums up idea of change — refers to the wording of the task.

Student X just succeeds in delivering a clear and sustained focus on the task in terms of content (Elizabeth's changing impression) and style (how Austen communicates this). He or she attempts to get to grips with language (emotive words, irony) as well as narrative methods such as dialogue and letters. Generally, Student X avoids storytelling and selects clear supporting evidence from the text.

This stays at grade 5 because analysis is straightforward, with some minor misinterpretation; also the references to context lack development. There are some instances of inappropriate style. However, as AO4 is not assessed, it will not significantly affect the overall mark.

Student Y addresses part 2 of the question like this, with more detail and more analysis of language:

1 Authorial method identified and then explored (AO2).

When Wickham next meets Elizabeth at her aunt's gathering, Austen makes extensive use of dialogue to show how articulate and persuasive he can be, and how he shows himself in a good light by gaining sympathy both from the reader and Elizabeth. He begins by fuelling her prejudice against Darcy in an emotive manner, claiming that 'the world is blinded by his fortune and consequence, or frightened by his high and imposing manners'. Austen's use of antithetical (like this) and triple sentence structures further deceives the reader, since Wickham not only looks like, but also speaks like an educated gentleman. Encouraged by Elizabeth's response, he continues in this negative vein to imply that he has been hard done by, a 'disappointed man' as the church 'ought' to have been his profession. Her reaction is also a triple of emotive condemnation of Darcy: 'such malicious revenge, such injustice, such inhumanity'. The sympathy of the reader for the one and dislike of the other is reinforced.

2 Insightful and sustained analysis of stylistic significance of judiciously chosen evidence (AO1 and AO2).

3 Skilfully integrated quotations — sustained focus on the question and on function of linguistic devices (AO1 and AO2).

1 Specific and relevant summary of complex content (AO1).

2 Linked with detailed knowledge about historical context (AO3).

He relates how the late Mr Darcy intended to 'provide amply' for him with a 'valuable living'. This is very significant, because it was normally the second son of a wealthy family who was given the opportunity to enter the church. However, Wickham was merely the son of one of the employees on the estate, so this was a real act of generosity. When he claims that Darcy denied him this promise because of 'a dislike which I cannot but attribute in some measure to jealousy', Elizabeth's point of view influences the reader to surmise that this may well be the truth. However, Austen provides plenty of linguistic clues here that Wickham caused his own problems: he says Darcy accused him of 'extravagance, imprudence — in short anything or nothing' (another triple) and confesses to a 'warm unguarded temper' and, though these are fairly abstract as descriptions of faults, they later turn out to be the cause of Darcy's decision not to honour his father's promise. Elizabeth, however, is shown to be blind to these clues, partly as she finds Wickham very attractive: his 'very countenance may vouch for [his] being amiable'. She also fails to recognise how inappropriate such intimate revelations are to a person he hardly knows, largely because of her prejudice against Darcy.

3 Perceptive inference and analysis with good use of apt short quotations (AO1 and AO2).

1 Clear understanding of the purpose and effect on the plot of the letters (AO2).

Damning information about Wickham is communicated in letters, a technique Austen uses to propel her narrative from a variety of different first person viewpoints. Darcy's letter reveals the truth: Wickham rejected the offer of a career in the church and chose to study law, then wasted the £3,000 given him by Darcy on 'a life of idleness and dissipation' instead of spending it on his studies. We also learn that Miss King is not the first heiress to tempt Wickham, for he planned an elopement with Georgiana Darcy when she was only 15 years old.

2 Good example of Austen's use of comparative details.

Elizabeth is shamed and embarrassed about her poor judgement of character, thus tells no one except Jane about this, so warning signs are missed when Lydia is allowed to follow Wickham's regiment to Brighton. Two letters from Jane to Elizabeth reveal that Wickham and Lydia have eloped to Scotland, then, even worse, that they are unmarried and living together in London. Add this to his pursuit of Miss King and Georgiana she now has good reason to see Wickham as an unscrupulous villain. Fortunately, Darcy finds them and the couple are married. This is a huge relief to Elizabeth as the scandal would have made the whole family social outcasts at that time, not to speak of the consequences for Lydia, who may well have slipped into a life of prostitution, as there would have been little hope of any other future for her once Wickham lost interest. Austen does not make a point like this explicitly, but any contemporary reader would have known the likely consequences.

3 Authorial methods identified and structure of plot considered (AO1 and AO2).

4 Sophisticated grasp of social and historical context (AO3).

The complete tale of Wickham's moral evil is not revealed until Mrs Gardiner's letter communicates what Darcy paid Wickham to marry Lydia: his debts paid 'amounting…to considerably more than a thousand pounds, another thousand…settled on her and his commission purchased'.

5 Well-chosen textual detail summarised to make a precise point (AO1).

Student Y concludes like this:

1 Highlights authorial method (AO2) supported by apt quotation (AO1).

> Austen concludes with authorial comment, summing up the life Wickham goes on to lead. He soon loses interest in Lydia ('affection...sunk into indifference'), but retains the hope, despite all the evil he has done, and all he already owes to Darcy, that 'Darcy might yet be prevailed upon to make his fortune.' Their 'extravagant' and 'heedless' lifestyle leads them to depend on Elizabeth and Darcy for money and Bingley and Jane for somewhere to live.
>
> Wickham is a perfect illustration of the theme of how deceptive appearances can be. Austen's method of allowing the reader to uncover the depths of his villainy from the viewpoint of Elizabeth and to share her condemnation of the man who initially struck her as 'completely charming' is an interesting aspect of the novel. He ends, as he began, as a total contrast to Darcy, whose good qualities are emphasised by the comparison.

2 Conclusion illustrates clear focus on requirement of task — ranging over whole text, exploring links between events and themes and sustaining an appropriate critical style (AO1).

This response combines a complex discussion of Wickham's character with investigation of Austen's style and authorial method. The answer is focused, logical and fluently expressed. Textual evidence — quotation and reference — supports all points made, and there is fine-tuned analysis and evaluation of both content and language. There is also a good critical grasp of authorial methods, such as point of view, irony, dialogue and letters.

There is detailed and relevant comment on social and historical context. In addition, Student Y alludes to several of the themes in the novel, though this is not specifically required by the question. This essay demonstrates a conceptualised overview of the whole text. Overall, this merits a good grade 8.

Eduqas sample question and response

Eduqas questions are similar to AQA questions: the task is extract-based and may involve exploring character, relationships, structure of the novel or themes. The wording of the task directs you to discuss **the extract** as well as your **knowledge of the whole novel** and specifically asks you to **refer to contexts**, as AO3 gains a third of the available marks on this exam. The question below is a theme-based example. Equal marks (13+) are awarded for AO1, AO2 and AO3; no marks are awarded for AO4 on this question.

Pride and Prejudice

You are advised to spend about 45 minutes on this question.

You should use the extract below and your knowledge of the whole novel to answer this question.

Write about attitudes to marriage in *Pride and Prejudice* and how they are shown in the novel.

In your response you should:

- refer to the extract and the novel as a whole;
- show your understanding of characters and events in the novel;
- refer to the contexts of the novel.

[40 marks]

'Engaged to Mr. Collins! my dear Charlotte, — impossible!'

The steady countenance which Miss Lucas had commanded in telling her story, gave way to a momentary confusion here on receiving so direct a reproach; though, as it was no more than she expected, she soon regained her composure, and calmly replied,

'Why should you be surprised, my dear Eliza? — Do you think it incredible that Mr. Collins should be able to procure any woman's good opinion, because he was not so happy as to succeed with you?'

But Elizabeth had now recollected herself, and making a strong effort for it, was able to assure her with tolerable firmness that the prospect of their relationship was highly grateful to her, and that she wished her all imaginable happiness.

'I see what you are feeling,' replied Charlotte, — 'you must be surprised, very much surprised, — so lately as Mr. Collins was wishing to marry you. But when you have had time to think it all over, I hope you will be satisfied with what I have done. I am not romantic, you know. I never was. I ask only a comfortable home; and considering Mr. Collins's character, connections, and situation in life, I am convinced that my chance of happiness with him is as fair as most people can boast on entering the marriage state.'

Elizabeth quietly answered 'Undoubtedly;' — and after an awkward pause, they returned to the rest of the family. Charlotte did not stay much longer, and Elizabeth was then left to reflect on what she had heard. It was a long time before she became at all reconciled to the idea of so unsuitable a match. The strangeness of Mr. Collins's making two offers of marriage within three days, was nothing in comparison of his being now accepted. She had always felt that Charlotte's opinion of matrimony was not exactly like her own, but she could not have supposed it possible that, when called into action, she would have sacrificed every better feeling to worldly advantage. Charlotte the wife of Mr. Collins, was a most humiliating picture! — And to the pang of a friend disgracing herself and sunk in her esteem, was added the distressing conviction that it was impossible for that friend to be tolerably happy in the lot she had chosen.

Student X, who is likely to achieve grade 5, begins as follows:

In Jane Austen's time, marriage was an important aspect in life for many reasons. Marriage was one of women's main aims to provide them with independence from their parents with 'a comfortable home' of their own, which Charlotte Lucas mentions in this extract. Charlotte's engagement to Mr Collins is the focus, but the whole novel also shows contrasts in attitudes to marriage especially from Elizabeth Bennet who eventually marries Mr Darcy and the badly judged match between Lydia and Wickham.

One of the worst marriages in literature has to be Charlotte and Mr Collins. They have nothing at all in common. Charlotte is presented as being quite clever and sensible, whilst Collins seems to be a complete idiot, frankly! In this extract we see a massive difference of opinion between Charlotte and Elizabeth. Their dialogue and Austen's use of authorial comments show the intelligence of these women as they both reflect on Charlotte's surprise engagement. Elizabeth

1 Clear focus on the task in opening sentence (AO1) and a nod at historical context (AO3).

2 Relevant detail from the extract and clear comment on both the extract-based and whole novel aspects of the task (AO1).

3 Register less formal than appropriate, but does indicate strong personal involvement in the text (AO1).

4 Clear comment on language (AO2).

5 Relevant quoted detail (AO1) and understanding of specific language devices (AO2).

6 Clear commentary on specific language device.

says very little, which is unusual for her. Her outburst of 'impossible' is quite rude, but she controls herself enough to say Charlotte will 'Undoubtedly' have as much chance of happiness as anyone getting married. This comment is probably irony as the final paragraph is mainly narrated from her point of view and shows her thinking about 'the strangeness of Mr Collins's making two offers of marriage in three days', the first of which she herself had refused. Charlotte was her best friend, but Elizabeth thinks she is 'disgracing herself and sunk in her esteem.' These are lists and almost like triples. This is a technique Austen uses to show someone who is intelligent and thoughtful. Austen uses Elizabeth's point of view to show her attitude that it is 'so unsuitable a match' and 'impossible for her friend to be tolerably happy', but that is really because she is judging from what she would want for herself.

Student X continues:

1 Good knowledge of the text and relevant evidence selected (AO1) and clear explanation of contrasting attitudes (AO2).

2 Commentary on use of specific language devices (AO2).

3 Understanding of historical context (AO3).

Charlotte sees Mr Collins as her one and only chance: 'I am not romantic, you know; I never was.' She is presented as down-to-earth and realistic — she wishes to marry for a roof of her own over her head, and she says she feels that 'Mr Collins' character, connections and situation in life' make him a good choice. (He is a clergyman and he will eventually inherit Longbourn from Mr Bennet.) Austen uses a triple in this speech, as she often does, to show Charlotte's intelligence. She says she felt that her 'chance of happiness with him is as fair as most people can boast on entering the marriage state.' Like Elizabeth she is using a lot of abstract nouns because this is an intellectual discussion.

Earlier in this chapter Austen uses her narrative point of view to tell the reader Charlotte's thoughts that explain why she accepts Mr Collins even though she knows it will be a big problem for her friendship with Elizabeth. Charlotte is plain and 27 years old, too old to marry in the nineteenth century, but this does not matter to Mr Collins as the main reason he is trying to find a wife is because Lady Catherine told him to.

Student Y's response, which addresses several similar points, begins:

Jane Austen wrote 'Pride and Prejudice' in the late eighteenth century, and the novel was published in the early 1800s. People then, especially the upper classes, had a very different perception of marriage from the one we have today: upper-class marriage was often more of a business arrangement than a romantic gesture, as the couple, and their families, had to take into consideration things such as money and social standing, often more so than love. Austen engages her reader in a debate by presenting us with a wide spectrum of attitudes to marriage. The extract shows a stark contrast between Elizabeth Bennet and her friend Charlotte Lucas. Later in the novel another extreme is presented in the attitude of Elizabeth's sister Lydia. Out of all the perspectives, these three will be my main focus.

In this extract there are two key words — 'unsuitable' and 'happiness'. What makes a marriage 'suitable' or 'unsuitable' is explored throughout the novel. Whether or not a marriage is destined to bring happiness to a couple is also revisited. Austen presents a difference of opinion between Charlotte and Elizabeth by combining dialogue and shifting viewpoints to convey their debate to the reader. Elizabeth says very little, which is unusual: her initial reaction to news of Charlotte's engagement is an emotional outburst of 'impossible'. This is insulting, and also ambiguous as it is not entirely clear whether she is thinking of the recent proposal she herself has had from Collins, or the unlikelihood of acceptance by any woman of such a 'conceited, pompous, narrow-minded silly man', as she later describes him — an emotive list of his defects. That her best friend, who she judges to be 'sensible' would be so foolish is shown to be much on her mind, though Austen summarises her good wishes, saying that the match is 'highly grateful to her', conveying Elizabeth's approval, and her wish of 'all imaginable happiness'. This, like her terse final comment that Charlotte will 'Undoubtedly' have as much chance of happiness as anyone getting married mirrors the cynicism of her own father — ironically implying that marriage is unlikely to bring happiness to anyone.

1 Assured grasp of the social and historical context of the novel (AO3).

2 Begins with an overview of the task — apt topics for discussion chosen. Register appropriate for a literary essay (AO1). Indicates awareness of how contrast is used to structure the novel (AO2).

3 Assured identification of authorial methods with precise use of literary and linguistic terms (AO2) supported by pertinent quotation from the text (AO1).

4 Sustained evaluative comment on effects of language (AO2).

Student Y continues:

Charlotte's spoken words contrast with the emotion shown by Elizabeth: she seems to speak with the voice of Augustan 'reason', keeping her feelings under control: 'I am not romantic, you know; I never was.' She is presented as practical and realistic — she wishes to marry firstly for 'a comfortable home' and then says that 'Mr Collins's character, connections and situation in life' make him a suitable choice. The triple, as often in Austen's writing, reflects Charlotte's balance and intelligence. She continues with the opinion that her 'chance of happiness with him is as fair as most people can boast on entering the marriage state.' Later she reiterates the opinion that 'happiness in marriage is entirely a matter of chance', a view that Elizabeth cannot share, though Charlotte ends the conversation with the hope that Elizabeth will 'think it over' and 'be satisfied.' The reader understands that Charlotte is plain and in her late twenties, which would make her unlikely to be chosen as a bride by many men at that time. Mr Collins is her only chance: their marriage is for convenience and security, thus she is prepared to marry a man who she is in no way attracted to and cannot even respect.

1 Sophisticated comment on the cultural context on this text (AO3).

2 Evaluative commentary on language continues (AO2) with apt reference both to the extract and the whole text (AO1).

3 Assured understanding of historical and social context (AO3).

Student X addresses the theme in the wider novel:

1 Clear explanation of another contrasting attitude with language in focus (AO2).

Elizabeth's marriage might be judged by some characters in the novel as 'unsuitable', for example the difference in social class is Lady Catherine's big objection 'to a young woman of inferior birth, of no importance in the world, and wholly unallied to the family!' She shows her education in this use of a triple and she also shows what a snob she is.

I think this is Austen's idea of a perfect marriage. In the nineteenth century the upper class mainly had arranged marriages, like Lady Catherine wanted between Darcy and his cousin Anne, keeping all the money in the family. Elizabeth takes a long time to overcome her prejudice that Darcy is a proud and cruel man and to discover that he is exactly the right man for her. The whole story shows how real love develops between Elizabeth and Darcy. Both of them learn from each other how to be better people. He loved her almost from the start of the story, but he has to see how his pride about his status is a barrier to being together. Theirs is the ideal marriage because they have love, they have companionship and they have financial security too, because Darcy is very rich. This is important to their future happiness. Austen seems to suggest that marrying just for money is not a good basis for marriage, but marrying without even thinking about money is foolish too.

2 Clear comment on historical and social context (AO3).

3 Shows insight into the structure of the plot (AO2).

Student Y moves on to address the wider novel like this:

It is clear that a compromise of this sort would not suit Elizabeth who thinks it is 'so unsuitable a match' and 'impossible for her friend to be tolerably happy', implying that she has different aspirations.

The whole issue of what is a 'suitable' match and what is not is central to this theme. Some might say that the difference of social class and wealth between Elizabeth and Darcy make theirs an 'unsuitable' marriage, as Lady Catherine and even Darcy himself (the first time he proposes to her) state explicitly. What Austen seems to communicate by writing from Elizabeth's perspective is an ideal. Perhaps she is suggesting a balance between the logical perspective of the 'age of reason' with the new emphasis of Romanticism, where emotions were judged to be purer and more worthwhile as motivations for decisions. Elizabeth is portrayed as looking for a husband she can respect and consider an intellectual equal. Only her prejudice against Darcy prevents her from seeing that he is the one until near the end of the novel. By the end, the reader is in no doubt that real love, attraction and intellectual companionship has developed between this couple, and they have grown into better people because of it. Her father fears that she is marrying for 'worldly advantage', reminding us of Charlotte as he asks outright 'will this make you happy?' He is somewhat reassured when she says 'I love him' but goes on to emphasise how important it is to 'esteem' and 'respect' one's spouse, one reason why this marriage is such a contrast with Charlotte's, and introduces another perspective on what is 'suitable'.

1 Clear overview as the discussion contrasts two points of view (AO1).

2 Evidence of sophisticated grasp of cultural and literary context (AO3).

3 Excellent summary but the limited textual detail means that AO2 is not covered here.

4 Excellent textual knowledge (AO1) and a clear awareness of structural links (AO2).

Student X concludes in this way, rather briefly:

> I found this whole theme interesting.
> I think Jane Austen is making a point about marriage and showing the reader that even though status and financial security were important then, as well as the social classes you were marrying into, a marriage cannot be happy without love and companionship. At least Charlotte and Mr Collins have ~~similar~~ status and a steady income. Lydia and Wickham have none of these so their marriage is probably the most unsuitable one in the book.

1 Task remains in focus (AO1) and historical context (AO3).

2 In the full answer the marriage of Lydia and Wickham is also discussed — as indicated in the introduction.

Overall comment on Student X's response

In this grade 5 answer, the key word is 'clear'. It focuses on the task set and makes relevant comment on how the content of the text as a whole presents aspects of a central theme. It generally manages to avoid storytelling, and demonstrates an awareness of Austen constructing the text. There is relevant evidence from the text to support the points. Expression occasionally lapses into inappropriate informality, but in the main there is clear communication of ideas.

AO1 is stronger than AO2 and AO3, as the level of commentary on language and context at times demonstrates less secure understanding of more complex aspects of the text. Even so, these AOs are addressed throughout the answer, which is focused and sustained, so this would not lower the grade overall.

Student Y concludes more fully:

> The theme of marriage (and its close links with money) is central to 'Pride and Prejudice' from the opening statement. Austen's didactic purpose is to the fore as she makes use of characters like those discussed above to show her readers that even though issues of social status and financial security were important in considering 'suitability' of a partner, a marriage cannot bring lasting happiness without love, and the kind of personal compatibility that leads to an equal companionship. Austen's successful marriages give a couple a solid basis for their future family life. Marriages of convenience like that of Charlotte and Mr Collins succeed to an extent because there is compatibility in having similar status and the security of a steady income. Marriages like Lydia and Wickham's are destined to fail, having none of the compatability necessary to support lasting happiness.

1 Authorial methods remain in focus (AO2).

2 In the full answer the marriage of Lydia and Wickham is also discussed — as indicated in the introduction.

3 Overview of the text (AO1) and evaluation of structure in terms of use of contrast (AO2) as the task is concluded.

Overall comment on Student Y's response

This considered response reaches grade 8 combining as it does a discussion of this key theme with perceptive comment on aspects of the contemporary context of the novel. Throughout there is evidence of a detailed knowledge of the whole text and of the narrative devices Austen employs. Restricting the focus of discussion to just 3 contrasting attitudes to marriage means that the argument is very well-structured and evidence is apt and well integrated into the answer, skilfully exploring parallels and contrasts in a conceptualised response.

Top ten

As your examination will be 'closed book' and you will only have a short extract in front of you, you might find it helpful to memorise some short quotations to use in support of your points in the examination response.

Top ten characterisation quotations
Miss Elizabeth Bennet

Louisa: '...She really looked almost wild.'
Caroline: 'Her hair so untidy, so blowsy!'
Louisa: '...her petticoat, six inches deep in mud...' (Ch. 8, p. 30)

1

- When Elizabeth arrives at Netherfield the Bingley sisters are shocked that she has walked two miles — a lady would arrive by carriage. Darcy contradicts them, saying the exercise has 'brightened' her eyes.

'There is a stubbornness about me...My courage always rises with every attempt to intimidate me.' (Ch. 31, p. 136)

2

- Whilst visiting Lady Catherine, Elizabeth admits this quality of hers to Darcy, highlighting her unconventional, rebellious streak.

...she checked herself. She remembered that he had yet to learn to be laughed at... (Ch. 58, p. 286)

3

- Austen narrates from Elizabeth's point of view, indicating to us that marriage to Darcy will temper her faults: her impetuous judgements and her over-ready wit.

GRADE *BOOSTER*

The most frequently used method for learning quotations is to write them down, repeat them and then test yourself. However, if you are a visual learner, you might try drawing a cartoon with the quotation as a caption.

Mr Fitzwilliam Darcy

4

Darcy was clever. He was at the same time haughty, reserved, and fastidious, and his manners, though well bred, were not inviting. (Ch. 4, p. 15)

- Authorial comment — the point of view of those present at the Meryton ball? Note use of triple and antithesis.

5

'...obstinacy is the real defect of his character...He has been accused of many faults..., but *this* is the true one.' (Ch. 52, p. 248)

- Mrs Gardiner's letter describes Darcy's determined efforts to find Lydia and Wickham. He and Elizabeth have similar aspects of character — see 2 above.

6

'I was spoiled by my parents...almost taught...to be selfish and overbearing...to think meanly of all the rest of the world.' (Ch. 58, p. 284)

- Darcy reflecting on his faults of character. Like Elizabeth, he realises that she can check negative aspects of his behaviour and make him a better person.

Miss Jane Bennet

7

'You never see a fault in anybody. All the world are good and agreeable in your eyes.' (Ch. 4, p. 14)

- Elizabeth's comment sums up Jane. This trait makes her gullible in certain situations, but it also means she will never fall into traps that Elizabeth's judgemental character make her prone to.

8

...whatever she felt she was desirous of concealing, and between herself and Elizabeth, therefore, the subject was never alluded to. (Ch. 23, p. 104)

- A rare opportunity to share Jane's point of view, highlighting her tendency to conceal her emotions. Here she hides her pain when Bingley leaves Netherfield.

Mr Charles Bingley

9

'He is just what a young man ought to be...sensible, good humoured, lively; and I never saw such happy manners! — so much ease, with such perfect good breeding!' (Ch. 4, p. 13)

- Jane's comment (note the triple) about Bingley after their first meeting perhaps says as much about her as about him (see 7 above).

'You are each of you so complying, that nothing will ever be resolved on; so easy, that every servant will cheat you; and so generous, that you will always exceed your income.' (Ch. 55, p. 268)

10

- Mr Bennet's concluding comment (again a triple) about Jane and Bingley shows their compatibility, but the cynical intensifiers ('so... so...so...') indicate their weaknesses.

Top ten moments

The story of the novel is the unfolding of the relationship between Elizabeth and Darcy. Here are ten key moments in that process (with bold font used to suggest shorter sections to memorise):

'**She is tolerable, but not handsome enough to tempt** *me*; and I am in no humour...to give consequence to young ladies who are slighted by other men.' (Ch. 3, p. 11–12)

1

- At the Meryton ball, Darcy callously insults Elizabeth in a most ungentlemanly way. His comment seals her dislike.

'I have been meditating on the very great pleasure which **a pair of fine eyes in the face of a pretty woman** can bestow.' (Ch. 6, p. 23)

2

- Darcy rapidly changes his opinion, showing that he is attracted to Elizabeth, thus provoking Caroline Bingley's jealousy.

'...though I have never liked [Darcy], I had not thought so very ill of him — I...**did not suspect him of descending to such malicious revenge, such injustice, such inhumanity as this!**' (Ch. 16, p. 65)

3

- Elizabeth's dislike of Darcy is furthered by Wickham's tale of ill treatment at his hands. Note the triple.

'In vain have I struggled. It will not do. My feelings will not be repressed.'...He spoke well; but there were feelings besides those of the heart to be detailed...**His sense of her inferiority** — of its being a degradation — of **the family obstacles**...were dwelt on with a warmth... [which] was very unlikely to recommend his suit. (Ch. 34, p. 147–48)

4

- Darcy's proposal of marriage to Elizabeth is a shock to her, but also further confirmation of his arrogance.

5 'From the very beginning...your arrogance, your conceit, and your selfish disdain of the feelings of others, were such as to form that ground-work of disapprobation, on which succeeding events have built so immoveable a dislike...**you were the last man in the world whom I could ever be prevailed on to marry**.' (Ch. 34, pp. 150–51)

- Elizabeth angrily rejects Darcy's offer of marriage.

> **GRADE** *BOOSTER*
>
> ```
> The memory part of your brain loves colour. Try
> copying these quotations out using different colours
> for different characters. You might organise them into
> mind maps or write them onto post-it notes and stick
> them around your room.
> ```

6 '...the effort which the formation, and the perusal of this letter must occasion, should have been spared had not **my character required it to be written and read**.' (Ch. 35, p. 153)

- Darcy's long letter defends his 'character' and good name against Elizabeth's accusations of ungentlemanly behaviour. The letter initiates changes in each as he reflects on his pride, she on her prejudice.

7 **She respected, she esteemed, she was grateful to him, she felt a real interest in his welfare**; and she only wanted to know...how far it would be for the happiness of both that she should employ the power...of bringing on the renewal of his addresses. (Ch. 44, p. 203)

- The change in Elizabeth's feelings is complete: visiting Pemberley, she reassesses Darcy on the basis of what she hears of him and sees of his estate — another triple.

8 She began now to comprehend that he was exactly the man who, in disposition and talents, would most suit her...**It was an union that must have been to the advantage of both**; by her ease and liveliness, his mind might have been softened, his manners improved; and from his judgment, information, and knowledge of the world, she must have received benefit of greater importance. (Ch. 50, p. 239)

- Lydia's elopement ends all hope for this relationship — here Elizabeth reflects remorsefully on her loss of an 'equal marriage'.

'...dearest, loveliest Elizabeth!...You taught me a lesson, hard indeed... but most advantageous. **By you I was properly humbled.** I came to you without a doubt of my reception. You shewed me how insufficient were all my pretensions to please a woman worthy of being pleased.' (Ch. 58, p. 284)

9

- Darcy makes it explicit to Elizabeth, and the reader, how her rejection of his proposal has changed him. This time she accepts.

'I do, I do like him...**I love him. Indeed he has no improper pride. He is perfectly amiable.** You do not know what he really is...' (Ch. 59, p. 290)

10

- Elizabeth shares her feelings with the reader as she reassures her father that she is marrying Darcy for love rather than for his wealth and position, and that she will be happy in this marriage.

GRADE *BOOSTER*

Another useful method of memorising quotations is to record them onto your iPod and play them over and over. Or you might try watching one of the many adaptations to spot where a quote appears. This can be an effective method as you have both sound and vision to help you, and you can see the quotation in context of the performance.

Top ten thematic quotations
Pride

Mrs Bennet: '...every body says that he is eat up with pride, and I dare say he had heard somehow that Mrs. Long does not keep a carriage...'
Charlotte: 'His pride...does not offend *me* so much as pride often does... so very fine a young man, with family, fortune, everything in his favour ... has a *right* to be proud.'
Elizabeth: 'That is very true...and I could easily forgive *his* pride, if he had not mortified *mine*.' (Ch. 5, pp. 17–18)

1

- Note the range of opinions: for Mrs Bennet, Darcy's pride is simple social snobbery; Charlotte looks for a justification for his lack of interaction; Elizabeth shows insight and the ability to laugh at her own folly as she identifies how Darcy hurt her feelings.

2 Georgiana's reception of them was...attended with all that embarrassment which, though proceeding from shyness,...would easily give to those who felt themselves inferior the belief of her being proud and reserved. (Ch. 45, p. 204)

- Authorial comment: Mrs Gardiner and Elizabeth witness how Georgiana's shyness might be misinterpreted — parallels with her brother are implicit.

3 'As a child...I was given good principles, but left to follow them in pride and conceit...I was spoiled by my parents, who...almost taught me...to care for none beyond my own family circle...' (Ch. 58, p. 284)

- Darcy explains to Elizabeth how he has come to understand, and overcome, his improper pride. The impact of upbringing is emphasised here.

Prejudice

4 *Darcy:* 'I cannot forget the follies and vices of others...nor their offences against myself....My temper would perhaps be called resentful. — My good opinion once lost, is lost for ever.'
Elizabeth: '...you have chosen your fault well. I really cannot *laugh* at it; you are safe from me.' (Ch. 11, p. 47)

- Darcy and Elizabeth debate faults of character. Note the elegant triple with which Darcy builds up to the identification of his admission, indicating his intellect and education.

5 Of neither Darcy nor Wickham could she think without feeling that she had been blind, partial, prejudiced, absurd. '...vanity, not love, has been my folly...I have courted prepossession and ignorance, and driven reason away...Till this moment, I never knew myself.' (Ch. 36, p. 162)

- Elizabeth's moment of anagnorisis (see page 23) as she reflects on Darcy's letter and tells Jane that her prejudiced judgements have clouded her intellect.

6 'I am no stranger to the particulars of your youngest sister's infamous elopement...And is *such* a girl to be my nephew's sister? Is *her* husband, who is the son of his late father's steward, to be his brother?...Are the shades of Pemberley to be thus polluted?' (Ch. 56, p. 275)

- Lady Catherine shows the prejudice of social class by objecting to Elizabeth's marrying into her higher-ranking family. This is exaggerated to the point of satire as she lists everything hurtful she can think of — culminating in the offensive (and amusing) alliterative comment at the end.

Marriage

'...if you take it into your head to go on refusing every offer of marriage in this way, you will never get a husband at all — and I am sure I do not know who is to maintain you when your father is dead. — *I shall not be able to keep you...*' (Ch. 20, p. 91)

7

- The link between marriage and finance could not be made clearer: Mrs Bennet berates Elizabeth for refusing Collins — thus losing the opportunity to keep Longbourn in the Bennet family.

'...what is the difference in matrimonial affairs, between the mercenary and the prudent motive?...you were afraid of his marrying me, because it would be imprudent; and now, because he is trying to get a girl with only ten thousand pounds, you want to find out that he is mercenary.' (Ch. 27, p. 120)

8

- Again the link between marriage and finance. Elizabeth discusses Wickham's pursuit of an heiress with her aunt, Mrs Gardiner.

Parents/family relationships

Elizabeth...had never been blind to the impropriety of her father's behaviour as a husband. She had always seen it with pain...that continual breach of conjugal obligation and decorum which, in exposing his wife to the contempt of her own children, was so highly reprehensible. (Ch. 42, p. 183)

9

- The failings of the Bennets' marriage and parenting is constantly reiterated — sometimes from the authorial perspective (Ch. 1, p. 7), occasionally from Mr Bennet's own reflections (Ch. 50, p. 236) and here from Elizabeth's point of view.

...a family so deranged, a father absent, a mother incapable of exertion, and requiring constant attendance... (Ch. 46, p. 214)

10

- Authorial comment on the inept parenting of Mr and Mrs Bennet after Lydia elopes, which includes yet another triple.

Wider reading

Other novels by Jane Austen

You could read, or watch a film version of, another of Austen's novels. *Sense and Sensibility* also has two sisters as contrasting main characters. *Emma* provides an excellent opportunity to consider how Austen constructs a plot from the point of view of an unreliable narrator.

Sequels

Most readers are left wondering 'what happened next?', and several modern authors have written sequels to the novel. You might enjoy *Pemberley* and *An Unequal Marriage* by Emma Tennant, and P.D. James' *Death Comes to Pemberley* uses the original characters and setting as the inspiration for a gripping detective story, also adapted for television.

Graphic versions

Though no substitute for reading the original to prepare for your exam, if you enjoy graphic novels, you could read the Manga Classics version of *Pride and Prejudice* (Udon Entertainment 2014) alongside the novel.

Non-fiction

- Janet Todd: *Jane Austen: Her Life, Her Times, Her Novels* (Andre Deutsch Ltd, 2013) is an informative and beautiful book, containing some facsimile documents from Austen's times.
- Christopher Ghillie: *A Preface to Jane* Austen (Routlege, revised edition 2014) gives contextual information and critical analysis of *Pride and Prejudice* and Austen's other novels.

Useful websites

- pemberley.com — one of the best websites for researching Austen or her writing. A hyperlinked online text of *Pride and Prejudice* is here as well as biographical information about Austen and film adaptations of the novel.
- www.jane-austens-house-museum.org.uk — a great place to visit to find out more about Austen's life.
- www.bbc.co.uk/drama/prideandprejudice — clips from the BBC 1995 TV series.
- YouTube — there are tens of thousands of clips from television and film adaptations here, including full productions of some films.

Answers

Answers to 'Review your learning' questions

Context (p. 15)

1   The context of a novel includes the social, historical, cultural and literary factors which influenced the author, and the ways different readers respond to the novel in different times and places.

2   In the early 1800s, although there had been female novelists, the work of very few women was published. Generally, it was not considered appropriate for women.

3   The Regency period was named for the Prince Regent, who ruled England from 1811, when his father, George III, was declared insane, until his death in 1820. The term is used for the time between the Georgian and the Victorian age: mid 1790s to 1830s.

4   The Romantic movement was a reaction against earlier ideas which emphasised the importance of reason. Romantic literature, art philosophy stressed the importance of emotion and the power of the natural world.

5   Entailment is a form of inheritance where there is no direct male heir in a family, so the estate passes to the nearest male relative.

6   Women in the nineteenth century did not generally own wealth and property, so they had to marry to ensure financial independence from their family. Younger sons did not usually inherit large fortunes, so they too had to look for a dowry (or settlement) when choosing a wife.

7   A marriage based on romantic love is Jane Austen's contribution to the genre of romantic fiction. For that reason, the novel has a timeless appeal. The issue of parents wishing to find suitable husbands for their daughters still has relevance to some British communities.

Plot and structure (p. 27)

1   Late summer/early autumn; the novel begins in September and ends in October the following year.

2   Obstables include: Elizabeth's initial dislike of Darcy; the social distance between his and her families; rivals for her affection; Wickham's lies about Darcy; Darcy's decision to separate Bingley from Jane; Lydia's elopement; Lady Catherine's disapproval.

3   Rivals for the heroine's affections are a typical feature of a romantic novel. Mr Collins shows that Elizabeth is not so desperate that she would accept anyone's proposal; Wickham represents a charmer, who turns out to be a villain; Darcy's cousin, Colonel Fitzwilliam, is a genuine rival whose attentions to Elizabeth make Darcy jealous, but his circumstances mean the relationship has no future.

4   Elizabeth falls in love with Darcy when she visits Pemberley (Ch. 42) in July.

5   The Gardiners are Elizabeth's means of visiting Darcy's estate at Pemberley. They show that high social class is not the only source of culture and good breeding. In contrast to the Bennets' ineffective parenting, at several times in the novel they take on a parental role for Elizabeth, Jane and Lydia.

6   Both Lydia and Georgiana are victims of Wickham. His plans to elope with Georgina are discovered and prevented. However, he succeeds with Lydia.

7   The seasons over the year of the novel act as a symbol for characters' emotions: after an action-packed autumn, the winter months are quiet and slow, reflecting the unfulfilled hopes of Jane (with Bingley) and Elizabeth (with Wickham); Easter brings new hope as Darcy proposes to Elizabeth and her feelings towards him begin to grow; in the summer, love blooms at Pemberley; the double marriage of Jane and Elizabeth comes in the autumn completing the cycle of the seasons.

Characterisation (p. 44)

1   Characters are presented by: conversation (dialogue) — what the character says (or thinks) and what others say about him/her; actions — what a character does; behaviour in a social setting — how he/she relates to others; authorial comment — how the author judges the character.

2   The three younger sisters are Mary, Kitty and Lydia. They are included as comparisons with Elizabeth. Lydia adds to the plot by eloping with Wickham. All have stereotypical aspects of female behaviour, which bring humour to the novel.

3   Mr Collins and Lady Catherine de Burgh are exaggerated caricatures. They add humour to the novel, but they also contribute to various themes (for instance by their pride).

4   Jane Bennet; Mr Darcy; Lydia Bennet; Anne de Bourgh

5   Caroline Bingley to Darcy, revealing her jealousy of his attention to Elizabeth; Mr Bennet to Mary, showing his witty cynicism as he draws attention to her awful piano playing.

6   Mrs Bennet to Elizabeth, showing how materialistic she is: she is not concerned about what her daughter feels for the man she has agreed to marry, simply that she will gain money and possessions from the match.

Themes (p. 55)

1   A theme is an idea or an issue that a writer chooses to explore.

2   The five themes identified are money and marriage, parenthood and family life, love and friendship, pride and prejudice and appearance and reality.

3   The title *Pride and Prejudice* is taken from *Cecilia*, a novel by Fanny Burney, which also explores this major theme.

4   The Bennets', the Lucases' and the Gardiners' are the main marriages used to illustrate the theme of family life.

5   Both the characters of Darcy and Wickham demonstrate that appearances may be deceptive.

6   The theme of marriage is closely connected with money because the two were very much linked at the time Austen was writing. Although the novel shows that the ideal involves love, sound finances are non-negotiable as a basis for upper class marriage.

7   This will vary according to your opinion, but some of the themes relating to context may be difficult for a modern reader to grasp, such as the importance of money when marriage is considered. The theme of friendship and the love story that leads to Elizabeth and Darcy's marriage, however, have a timeless appeal.

Language, style and analysis (p. 66)

1   An epistolary novel is one made up entirely of letters between characters. *First Impressions*, an early draft of *Pride and Prejudice*, was written in this form. Around 40 letters are either mentioned, or included, in this novel.

2   Dialogue reveals characters through the subject matter and the style of speech. Mr Bennet's witty cynicism is unmistakable. Collins' strange mixture of vanity and humility is also characteristic.

3   Techniques used to incorporate humour include exaggeration/caricature, satire and irony.

4   Rhetorical devices influencing Austen's sentence construction include triples, antithesis and litotes.

5   Although the novel is written in the third person, Austen, as **omniscient narrator**, at times chooses to interpret events through perceptions of different characters. When she writes ironically, there

are elements of **unreliable narration**. Letters provide more chances to include a variety of **first person viewpoints** such as Darcy's or Mrs Gardiner's.

6   Symbolism is to be found in the way the seasons reflect the development of the plot. The description of Pemberley also symbolises aspects of Darcy's character.

7   Instead of imagery, Jane Austen chooses vocabulary with great care and describes characters' actions, thoughts and reactions with well-constructed phrases, sometimes using contrasts, or specifying what is *not* the case about a character.

Tackling the exams (p. 75)

1   Paper 1 for AQA and OCR. Paper 2 for Edexcel and Eduqas.

2   No.

3   Only if you are sitting the OCR exam.

4   Between 45 and 55 minutes — check your exam board on page 68.

5   Quotations are a good way of supporting a point. They need not be long, and ideally should be embedded in your work.

6   No, unless you are sitting the OCR exam.

7   Planning will help you to organise your thoughts and avoid a muddle.

8   Check your work to make sure you have done your best.

Assessment Objectives and skills (p. 80)

1   There are four AOs.

2   AO1 assesses your understanding of the text and your ability to give evidence for your ideas.

3   AO2 requires comment about how the writer uses language, form and structure to create effects.

4   AO3 refers to the relationship between texts and the contexts in which they were written. AO3 receives no marks from Edexcel and the least marks from AQA and OCR on this question, but Eduqas gives it equal marks with AO1 and AO2.

5   AO4 refers to the accuracy of spelling, punctuation and grammar. Only OCR gives marks for AO4 for this question.

6   If you don't know this, find out from your teacher — and then look again at the table on page 68.

7   Do not: retell the story, quote at length, identify devices without explaining their effects, offer unsupported opinions, or write about characters as if they were real.